ENVIRONMENT
OF
VIOLENCE

ENVIRONMENT
OF
VIOLENCE

Readings of Cataclysm Cast in Stone

BY C. WARREN HUNT

POLAR PUBLISHING
CALGARY, ALBERTA, CANADA
1990

ISBN: 0-9694506-0-5
U.S. Library of Congress Catalog Number: 90-62569

Manufactured in the United States of America
By: Western Book/Journal Press
San Mateo, California 94403

Published by: POLAR PUBLISHING
P.O. BOX 4220 Station C
Calgary, Alberta
Canada, T2T 5N1

Canadian Cataloguing in Publication Data:
  Hunt, C. Warren (Charles Warren), 1924-
  Environment of Violence,
  Includes bibliographical references
  1. Historical geology.   I. Title   QE33.H86 1990   551.7   C90-090217

Dedicated To
JAPHETH HUNT
1711 - 1808

*Japheth Hunt's remarkable life
was dedicated to the founding of a nation on
constitutional principles, an experiment that had never been
tried by mankind.*

This book is dedicated to his memory.

TABLE OF CONTENTS

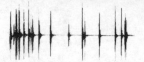

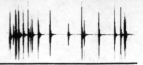

LIST OF ILLUSTRATIONS

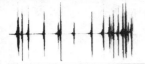

ENVIRONMENT OF VIOLENCE

READINGS OF CATACLYSM CAST IN STONE

A PROLOGUE

VASILIEVICH LOMONOSOV (1711-65) interpreted the geological processes of folding, rupturing, and uplift as imperceptibly slow. A generation later the famous Frenchman, Baron Cuvier, and the Englishman, James Hutton perceived in the rocks evidence of violent happenings, "catastrophes" they called them because of their portents for mankind. They recognized the gradual processes as did Lomonosov but considered them to be interrupted by violent events. Few of their contemporaries were ready to concede such ambivalent natural behavior.

In his early recognition of the importance of gradualism Lomonosov was far ahead of his contemporaries. In the words of S. Warren Carey,

> **"Small steps are acclaimed; large leaps are scorned.** A century was to pass before Europe reached Lomonosov's level of understanding of geological phenomena."
> Adapted from S. Warren Carey, 1988, THEORIES OF EARTH AND UNIVERSE: A History of Dogma in the Earth Sciences, p.45

In the late eighteenth-century "Enlightment" the hypothesis of uniformity was born. This was the idea that there should be similar behavior between past and present processes in nature, an application of Rousseau's "pure reason", inductive reasoning, that is to say. It was a deduction of *the way things "ought to be"* (in the absence of proof to the contrary.)

After another generation, in the 1830s, the most prominent geological figure from our retrospective point of view was Sir Charles Lyell (1798-1875). He is often spoken of as the "father of

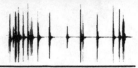

modern geology". More properly should Lomonosov have been mantled with that title. In any case, Lyell had vast influence, the deceased Lomonosov, little.

When Lyell, the lawyer, parliamentarian, and opinion maker, with thirteen friends started the London Geological Society as a "little talking dinner club" dedicated to promotion of liberal politics, its bias toward geology was an exploratory effort to find ultimate geological truth for the purpose of discrediting the political concept of the divine right of kings (Grinnell, 1976). If uniformity could be proved, the monarch's authority as the arbiter of change under natural law and, hence, of his credibility as God's interlocutor, would have been undermined.

Lyell's overpowering influence as a consequence of the success of his venture has evoked commentaries like the following:

> "All the hypotheses [with respect to landform development] that have reigned hitherto [are] confined by a limitation that originated with Lyell, namely, that *since there is no geologic repose on the face of the Earth, all surficial process must be (and must always have been) continuous*... an idea that has become a belief [and] an obstacle to clear thought. Lyell's axiom of continuing unending change ... is not much closer to the facts than was the older notion of geomorphic immutability" [the unchanging hills].
> From C.H. CRICKMAY, 1975, THE WORK OF THE RIVER, p249.

What resistance arose against Lyell's geological rationale occurred because of the corollary falsity that it imputed to the absolutes of the bible. Entrenched belief among the populace resulted in spirited defense of biblical dogma, defense which continues to this day on a diminished scale.

Lyell's mission was, therefore, discussion, not hammering rocks, a fact made easier because neither he nor any of his original cohorts was a geologist. The little politically-driven talking club grew rapidly, its later membership, dedicated to science, being little concerned over the imposture of politics associated with the founding.

Unlike the hot political topics of the day, which have faded (if not disappeared), the grandiose partial truth of universal gradualism still persists in many minds as immutable and exclusive

natural law. The effect has been pervasive, profound, and stifling for 160 years.

A century after Lomonosov's creative perception, and with Lyell having oversold his predecessor's idea as *"the"* all-pervasive geological truth, a younger generation undertook to apply gradualism to biological science. The young liberals, Herbert Spencer and Charles Darwin advanced natural selection to explain the origin of new life species. This concept had been proposed orginally by Erasmus Darwin, Charles' father, in 1794-96.

Darwin's prescription for evolution, which was to achieve immediate acclaim, was presented with words of patient tolerance for his anticipated detractors:

> **"Anyone whose disposition leads him to attach more weight to unexplained difficulties than to the explanation of a certain number of facts will certainly reject my theory".**
> From Charles A. Darwin, 1869, ORIGIN OF SPECIES.

It is my perception that the flight of pure reason that resulted in the dominance by Lyellian "uniformitarianism" of geology for 160 years symptomizes the results we should always expect from inductive reasoning unbridled by adequate field observation.

Geological science does not lend itself in its larger aspects to laboratory testing of hypotheses. The misconceptions that can be fostered by inductive resolution, as with the 160-year excursion over uniformity, will generally lead to dead ends or to monstrous nonsense. The public, relying on "expert opinion", is not encouraged to make its own observations, and few find the courage to "intrude" uninvited into the declared precincts of "experts" with anything so simple as common sense.

Bias against ideas not vetted and already held by "experts" is seldom carried in scientific journals and news magazines. "Experts" effectively screen out all but vetted hypotheses, which they already think they "know" and can treat as facts, expressing consensual satisfaction among themselves. Willingness to look anew into evidence supporting established doctrine is strangely anemic.

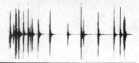

Darwin's proposal of natural selection was an extension of Lyellian gradualism, an integration of degradational, degenerative geological processes with progradational, regenerative life processes. Speciation as a function of response to environment, is a *degradational* function. Intended as a "uniform" theory of gradual change, the theory requires both geological and biological progress to move uni-directionally *from order toward disorder*.

Disquisition on Darwinism is beyond the context of this book. However, the relationship between ordered and disordered matter is not. To bring this into focus, let us pose a question: "Is there geological commonality to justify a theory of "uniformity" between life and geologic gradualism?"

If one defines life as a manifestation of order emerging from disorder, one's definition embodies the antithesis of the disorder that ensues from geological gradualism; and the answer to the question must be "no". A "no" answer negates either Darwinian natural selection or Lyellian gradualism.

But, if one finds geological order that emerges from chaos, one would have answered the question in the affirmative. Either life must be considered a degenerative process, or "inorganic" matter simulates life. The first violates the definitive quality of life, the ability to grow, to inculcate order where it had been absent. The second option must be our choice, therefore. Its implications are enormous.

The new science of fractals suggests the emergence of spontaneous order from chaos, a process that may operate in our universe and, perhaps, on Earth. In the coming pages I will show evidence that order does emerge from chaos in some geological situations, although, heretofore only life systems [carbon-containing systems] were recognized to be able to organize order out of randomness.

Now, if "inorganic" *carbon-free* materials are found able to organize themselves, *one is recognizing an astounding occurrence, inherent progenerative similarity between living and lifeless matter*. In the process one will have destroyed the Lyellian idea of exclusive degenerative gradualism as *"the"* all-encompassing principle of geology and will have established *a higher order linkage between organic and inorganic, life and non-life*.

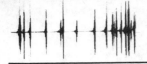

CONCEPT OF THIS BOOK

I will advance evidence for misfits between prevalent theory and observable fact, cases where little effort has been made to review long-standing, important, early ideas that have become entrenched and mislead us. I will present solutions, which I have developed over 45 years in the course of geological work and travel to work sites. Long drives, walks, horseback rides or flying trips are good times for thinking. Mainly, these have been in the American and Canadian west, but some have been elsewhere also. The scene has been a sort of never-ending unforgettable moving picture passing before my eyes. My thinking has spanned my career as a field geologist; the writing has had to await more leisurely years.

The problems dealt with in this book are of non-economic nature. However, my search for solutions to mineral and petroleum exploration problems has often allowed me time, and provided me with the evidence bearing on the non-economic problems. I take up the challenge of resolving enigmas and of writing a readable book with amusement and delight.

Conceptual solutions occur suddenly from a new angle of view or from new data. For example, some of my first field days in 1946 were spent close to the San Andreas fault in the Santa Cruz Mountains of northern California. My contribution to the enigma of the driving mechanism of that fault, as presented in this book, did not occur to me, however, until I was in the writing stage and the Loma Prieta earthquake of 1989 occurred directly beneath the site of my early field work. It so happened that the timing of the earthquake coincided with my formulation of a solution to the origin of the Klamath arc.

The extension of my Klamath solution to the San Andreas then was natural. *In my experience the leading obstacle to finding acceptable solutions to geological engimas, is predisposition toward respect for earlier authority. Again and again I have had the experience of following such prior authority, found myself in a blind alley, and had to backtrack painfully and start all over again.*

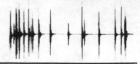

CATAFORM A NEW TERM

The term "cataform" is intended to define any geological relict created by a high-energy process. Creation in a very brief time-span is usual, since high energy dissipates quickly. But retrospective on short geological "events" can give false impressions of time.

The Cretaceous-Tertiary ("K/T") transition is an example of this. Accounted for by a metre or less of sediment makes it look short-lived. In reality, a 400,000-year timespan is represented by the sediment. The K/T "event" was hardly sudden, even to a geologist; and the asteroidal impact theory explaining it, as recently proposed (Alvarez, 1979), must be regarded as insufficient for that purpose.

Displacement with suddenness is the common characteristic of cataforms, not net energy release. Uniformitarian processes prevail by a large margin in transporting geological materials. Hyper-energetic, literally earth-shaking, cataclysmic events account for less, but they are in their time more dramatic. The intention of this book is to give a quantitatively sound perspective on the rarer violent features.

Cataform phenomena are incongruous with gradual geological regimens, the aberrance often standing out. On subsequent pages the reader will find a separation of cataforms into two main kinds, **first the primary cratering features affecting solid Earth and atmosphere,** and **then the secondary fluviatile cataforms.** Parts I and II respectively deal with these. Park III attempts to reconcile the magnitudes of the two varieties of cataform and to give some perspective on the timescales of repetition and the cause of the cataclysmic "events". Part IV takes up some enigmatic phenomena, which may with further investigation make the grade as cataforms.

Part I opens with discussion of known asteroidal cratering mechanisms and their cataforms, astroblemes, meaning "star-wounds", the scars left on Earth after meteorite impact. These "events" originate outside Earth, hence they are "exogenic". The counterpart to an exogenic crater, an astrobleme, is a crater originating from explosion from within the Earth, an "endogenic" feature.

A geologist named H. de la Rey Winter in a 1987 paper presented before the Workshop on Cryptoexplosions and Catastrophes in the Geological Record, South Africa, questioned the wisdom of interpreting the Vredefort crater feature of the central Witwatersrand basin as an astrobleme. Vredefort is the giant structure for which the term "astrobleme" was coined by the Canadian geologist, R. S. Dietz in 1961. Winter showed that the Vredefort structure is located at an intersection of major geological alignments and, hence, probably is endogenic in origin. He coined the term "gastrobleme," meaning "stomach wound" as a counter-term to astrobleme for this cataform. Curiously appropriate for the genera, this term is not yet in the dictionaries.

The true origin of Vredefort, as one can surmise from the above dichotomy, is extremely complex. Mountains of erudition have piled up on just that subject without resolving it. There seems to be about as much evidence for endogeny as for exogeny; and the subject will not be dealt with here in detail. Noteworthy, however, is the fact that meteorite impact possibly could have set off incipient explosive volcanism. This crater cataform may, thus, turn out to be a combination of exogeny and endogeny. In that scenario the major geological alignments that Winter points out may be legacies of endogeny triggered by exogeny.

Whereas astroblemes and gastroblemes are both cataforms, there are important contrasting features. Understanding of endogenic structures has lagged behind, while the space program has revealed an abundance of exogenic craters throughout the solar system. Over one hundred impact craters are recognized on Earth. By contrast, craters caused by mantle chamber explosion are hardly recognized at all. The efficacy of endogeny to produce a great cataform is discussed in connection with the Gros Brukkaros gastrobleme of Namibia and the Klamath Mountains cataform of California and Oregon.

Less cataclysmic than craters, but, nevertheless, hyperenergetic, are fluviatile cataforms. Products of inundation phenomena, these cataforms include steep-walled, flat-floored canyons, fields of broadcast boulders, erratics and other transported rock masses [known technically as "allocthons"]. A com-

mon characteristic of fluviatile cataforms is that they are secondary effects after primary endogeny or exogeny.

If, to use Darwin's expression, my hyper-energy theory of cataforms explains "a certain number of facts", science and readers will have been served as I intend.

THE SCOPE OF THIS BOOK

As a direct result of the space program in the 1960s, recognition swept over the scientific community that hyper-energy cometary impact processes operate disruptively throughout the Solar System. This recognition had the effect of emphatically negating gradualism as the exclusive agency of geological succession. Exogeny received much new attention from this time on, and the cataclysms of impacting bodies are now accepted as contributors in the creation of Earth's structural makeup.

The montage of construction and destruction that makes up the science of structural geology does not yield the secrets of the "gastroblemes" readily. I will try to present insights into these bizarre structures.

At about the same time as the space program was upsetting the apple cart of uniformitarian theory, followers of the Lyellian mode in geology have had to accept that the crust of the Earth is split by "spreading centers", where major additions of upwelling new rock are constantly arriving. Rising endogenously from Earth's interior, these crustal additions enter where pore pressure deficiencies allow their entry from below. They appear to have forced aside existing crust. But this appearance is probably an illusion; and the injections of crust on ocean floor or in continental rifts are more likely attributable to bouyancy of volatile-rich diapirs into chambers of deficient pressure. After reaching the surface, the emergent diapir may flow laterally, impelled by gravity and facilitated by repetitive internal recrystallization of minerals after the fashion of glacial ice and by mineral transformation into more-easily-sheared mineral fabrics, the serpentines and mylonites.

This creation of new crust is well-substantiated as a factual occurrence. Unfortunately, the theorists have built a pyramid of

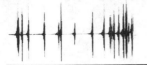

speculation that goes far beyond known fact. Theories of plate translation ["plate tectonics"] and of the downwelling of surface rock ["subduction"] are such important fabrications. Not based on much hard data, plate tectonics is, nevertheless, accepted widely, especially in North America.

The apparent spreading of the crust is taken to support downwelling ("subduction") to match upwelling of new material from below. A cooling-off process of the inner Earth is *taken for granted as necessary to preserve the constant circumference of the Earth.*

S. Warren Carey has pointed out the absence of hard evidence for either plate translations or subduction and the contrived nature of the "proof " that is advanced in their support. The prior assumption that something must descend into the crust to match that which has risen through it, is, in fact, unproven. On the contrary, subduction may be an unnecessary rationalization appended to proven crustal spreading.

In any case, as subduction does not provably occur, and as Carey's arguments have not been met, I will proceed without constraint to advance evidence for a much better explanation of the "few facts".

Returning now to Lyell's continuity axiom, which Crickmay (1975) amply disproved in the context of landform preservation (Part II), we should now recognize that Carey's hypothesis of a uni-directionally expanding Earth, if true, discredits the continuity axiom insofar as it is applicable to global tectonics. Instead of the winding-down process into which Lyell's theory leads us, Carey suggests an organization of order and emission of heat from unseen and uncomprehended inner Earth resources.

In my view the accepted version of the makeup of the Core and Mantle are due for major revision. Crustal materials as well as volatiles, water and petroleum especially, are being generated and extruded by unknown processes from unrecognized sources. Whether these phenomena can be shown to follow Newtonian physical principles or whether Newtonian physics is an inapplicable special case in a relativistic universe, we do not know. Perhaps relativity itself will prove to be a special case [Davies]; and the inner Earth may operate on exotic principles not yet imagined.

The universal condition explaining the growth of our planetary surface is not yet known, a state of affairs implying transience for today's conventional wisdom on the subject. Progradational [as opposed to degradational] processes still may prove the keys to geological endogeny.

The ancients thought of life as "creation". This was challenged as irrational in the age of reason of the eighteenth century. But it was not until the nineteenth century that anyone "progressed" to such an adumbration as the explanation of progenerative biological processes as analogs of degenerative geological processes. In theorizing that speciation is response to environment, Darwinian natural selection does just that, of course.

The legacy of natural selection theory has been a heavy baggage that has retarded intelligent thinking for one hundred thirty years. We may well be inclined to question the degree of enlightenment and pure reason behind the idea. But it must be remembered that only with the availability of space exploration and computer technology has science been able to gain any insight into the realms of chaos.

What we find are interesting orders that emerge spontaneously from chaotic states, higher energy forms [such as life] that arise from lower orders, patterned growth ["fractals"] coming out of disorder, and distinct levels at which pattern and new order materialize [Gleick, 1987].

Life itself, the prime example, is an impossible result to have emerged by random processes from a "primordial soup" [Hoyle]. More than the mechanistic sum of its parts, living matter has the capability of spontaneous organization from prior chaos [Margulis and Sagan], a capability emphatically impossible from random associations or gradual development.

Geological discrimination between the forces of endogeny or exogeny, deep Earth vs. deep space, is a first concern in this book. I will present site-specific microcosmic examples. These will be used as starting points from which satisfactory empirical solutions to local problems are possible. From there I will try to show the reader that my solutions, like Darwin's, are also based on a certain number of facts. And I will try to provoke a revolt against the desecration of Lomonosov's great idea by its over-extension in the hands of Lyell and Darwin.

If the reader reaches a more satisfactory perspective on the structure of the world around him, my purpose will have been served. Some new concepts found in this volume will not be found elsewhere. This is because they are new and heretical, and because I wish to present them without the inordinate delay and effective censorship that characterize the review process of scientific journals. An additional reason is that I want this book to be available to the general reader. For this purpose a Thumbnail Glossary for the Non-Geologist is included at the back.

Many aspects of geology today are still largely empirical science. The data base for inductive reasoning is made up of input that has alredy been filtered through someone's prejudgments as well as being quite limited. I think one should be wary of any theory not rooted in direct *geological* observation.

I hope the reader will find my solutions, which are founded on direct observation, to be comprehensible and devoid of the deficiencies inherent in indirect ("para-geological") observations and data juggling. I hope my fellow geologists will find insights they might otherwise not gain.

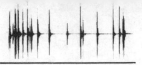

PART I

ASTROBLEMES, GASTROBLEMES, DIAPIRS AND DILATION

The Signatures of Impact, Explosion and Intrusion

Parkinson's rhetorical question as to what point it is in a man's life when his signature becomes illegible could as well be asked about circular features on the surface of the Earth. Where some people seem to have illegible signatures from birth, others inscribe tolerably well until they are buried. So it is with impact and explosion features: some distinct, others inscrutable.

Projectiles impacted into stable crystalline shield rock have produced craters visible for two billion years and more despite erosional wasting and the mantling effects of superdeposition. Impact craters in unstable terrain would be expected to be difficult or even impossible to detect soon after their creation. In the latter category one can imagine an impact in a near-shore ocean deep, where landslides could rapidly cover the evidence. Impact on a surface above rising magma, on the other hand, would also yield inscrutable results by triggering secondary volcanism and burying the evidence of impact. In the first case, the investigator is frustrated by lack of evidence; in the latter he is confronted with ambiguity between evidence for impact and for primary explosion.

RECENT EVENTS

The ultimate cataclysm imaginable to man has always been the stroke from heaven. Whether the stroke took the form of a comet, an ominous portent spelling disaster, martial defeat, pestilence or plague, or whether its form was the Jovian thunderbolt meting out destruction as divine punishment, heavenly caprice, or sport of

gods, the stroke of heaven has epitomized the image of calamity and has weighed heavily in the human psyche from earliest times.

By comparison with modern beliefs, mythology indicates ancestral concern for heavenly phenomena far outweighing anything known on Earth today. Even among the few remaining primitive tribes, there is little of this concern, a fact that seems incongruous with the alarmist attitudes of the builders of Stonehenge or the Great Pyramid at Giza. The early people seemed obsessed that celestial visitation would bring disaster. Comets in particular were thought to augur catastrophe.

The preoccupation of early man with celestial science is demonstrated in abundant folklore and religious ritual. Even with societies wholly separated from each other in distance or time, similar mythic themes are repetitively visible again and again worldwide. From continent to continent, culture to culture, and age to age in early times, remarkable similarities are found among myths. This seems to imply that links should be found to actual celestial events.

The implication is clear that prehistoric monument builders and early civilizations in general found more reason for being preoccupied with celestial events than modern people. Our indifference may reflect present-day lack of celestial spectacles that can be definitely associated with calamity.

In any case, attempts to resolve the origins of the myths of catastrophes past have led to elaborate analyses of prehistoric astronomies and related religious practices and cultures. These efforts have raised many intriguing questions but few answers. Equivocation rules the field.

The mythic "evidence" itself has not only failed to yield satisfactory answers, it has, in fact, brought on heated confrontation between innovators of new theories on ancient events and mainstream savants. The confrontation to end such confrontations was that known now as the "Velikovsky affair".

Immanuel Velikovsky, a psychiatrist by training, deduced heretical, outrageous and intriguing new correlations of archeological evidence involving aspects of astrophysics, archeology and geology. The basic theory Velikovsky advanced was that his interpretations of ancient texts indicated a different

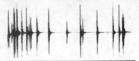

timetable for the ancient world and accommodated a near colli-sion between Earth and a wandering comet that later settled down as Venus. All manner of ancient legends were explained by this idea, or so he asserted.

The brouhaha that blew up embroiled factions from fundamen-talism to astronomy. The intricate interworkings of the heretic's theories defied complete negation despite one's knowledge that some parts of his ideas were nonsense. Thus, despite being innovative and creative, Velikovsky received the treatment of a para-scientific quack.

When the Velikovsky book, "Worlds in Collision", exploded on the 1950 literary scene unheralded by any prior contact with scientists, Velikovsky, arrogant and unwilling to admit error, found himself where he thought he deserved to be, in the global limelight.

Velikovsky's massive ego won him no sympathy in his incur-sions on the playing fields of science. The outrage he provoked resulted in some excellent analyses of the consequences of heresy in science and in the social aspects of "pure science," which turns out not to be so pure after all. The best comprehensive analysis of the "affair" is the book of Henry H. Bauer, *BEYOND VEL-IKOVSKY* (U. of Ill. Press, 1984).

The confrontations and antagonisms over the Velikovsky "af-fair" diverted attention of scientists from the scientific aspects of his pronouncements. But the attention of the public was engaged more securely than scientists had ever been able to engage it with their characteristic low profiles. And, when Velikovsky's intrigu-ing astrophysical predictions were substantiated, [if only in part and, as the scientists aver, for the wrong reasons], the consterna-tion of his critics only seemed to raise the inflammatory level of invective to a higher pitch.

The two most startling "successful" astrophysical predictions by Velikovsky were the magnetic field of Jupiter, and the high temperature of Venus' atmosphere. Having no conception of these conditions at the time Velikovsky forecast them, his detrac-tors derided them along with his other pronouncements. The critics were then dumbfounded and had to swallow their words and pride when the forecasts were confirmed by the space program in the 1960s.

However, few Velikovsky predictions have weathered so well. Others are demonstrably impossible, such as the absurdity of attribution of petroleum deposits to "snowstorms" of "manna" from heaven. Nevertheless, the several successes should have earned the author more than the derision and abuse he received.

For the purposes of this book it is clear that no large-scale impact phenomena in the last 6,000 years or so have been visited upon the Earth. Despite the veritable blizzard of new science over the last forty years, no evidence has emerged, geological or otherwise, to support Velikovsky's ideas of comets ejected from Jupiter, comet perturbations of planets or of a comet being converted to a planet. This is despite clever inductive scenarios contriving to justify the scientific possibility for such events.

The death of Velikovsky in 1979 softened the tone of the forty-year storm which he had triggered. Today, public awareness of the possibilities for new impact events is much enhanced. There is still an audience for anyone with a theory, heretical or otherwise, on the origin of myths of early man.

The beneficial infusion of the concepts of a nonconformist and the stimulation of current thinking that comes from an intrusion into the hallowed ground of "experts" is voluminously developed and recorded in print in connection with the Velikovsky affair.

I do not think the Velikovsky affair tells us much of science. Its lessons are about ourselves.

PROJECTILES FROM SPACE

Comets and Apollo Asteroids

Comets and large meteorites do strike the Earth and, not infrequently, they often pass close, sometimes giving us a celestial spectacle and a sense of relief at being missed. An example would be the October 31, 1936 passage of the two-billion-ton, three-km-diameter asteroid Hermes. It hurtled by Earth 770 000 km (480,000 mi.) distant, a near miss in astronomical terms. Impact would surely have destroyed most of civilization. A smaller but

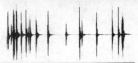

otherwise similar passage occurred March 23, 1989. This latter was never seen but was discovered on exposed film days later.

That makes one in about fifty years in our time. Were these events our only knowledge of such phenomena, the flux in earlier times would have a 50% probability of being either greater or less.

Grieve and Robertson of the Geological Survey of Canada have catalogued 116 impact craters worldwide and in sizes from .01 to 140 km in diameter. Myriad other circular structures are visible or implied by ringed geological features. These also may be relict impact craters. Most are too obscured by weathering and erosion to demonstrate clear impact character. In addition to known craters and the aforesaid myriad ringed features on the inhabited continental surfaces, large parts of Earth's land areas are either ice-covered, jungle-covered, or too little explored for the impact features to be visible or recognized.

Grieve and Robertson's 116 craters are all taken to be *asteroidal* impact sites. Most asteroids are thought to be the core relics of "burned-out" comets. No contrasting idea is current as to the difference one might expect between craters of true comets and their burned out cores, the asteroids.

Known Comet Impacts

Considering comets of "normal" type (mainly volatiles) in contrast to their burned-out meteoroidal cores, known impact sites are remarkably scarce. On June 30, 1908 an explosive occurrence known as the Tunguska event resulted from a fireball that streaked across the Siberian sky before exploding in mid-air. The consequences of the explosion of the missive include a report heard as far away as Leningrad and London, an airwave that encircled the Earth twice, a flattened forest, and people knocked off their feet sixty km distant. The only ground excavation comprised a cluster of pits each a few tens of metres in diameter. A rain of chondritic pellets showered the area. Aerosols from the explosion wafted around the world. No significant damage to human life or property occurred. The projectile, or "bolide", was

variously estimated to have had a mass of 1 to 7 million tonnes and a diameter of 300 to 500 metres before it detonated spontaneously. Kolesnikov (1988) has addressed the subject.

A second and very intriguing cometary event but one that is not commonly recognized is proposed by Mr. Mel Washkin, who develops the thesis that the Chicago fire of 1876 was actually caused by a small comet, "Mrs. O'Leary's comet", as he called it in his book by that name. This interesting idea is advanced and supported remarkably well by the daily press coverage and by fire department records. These reveal that many fires occurred, not just one. And the series of fires apparently commenced in villages to the north-northwest of Chicago and progressed to Chicago itself. Washkin reports interestingly on the apparent presence of pockets of gas in many sectors of the fire that would ignite spontaneously where there had been no fire before. These spontaneous fires created havoc with fire control efforts.

Icy Micro-Comets

A recent theorist, Louis Frank (1988) proposes that active impacting of icy "micro-comets" (3 to 5 m in diameter) is presently occurring in the upper atmosphere. Photography by physicist Clayne Yeates appears to confirm Frank's theory. Frank and Yeates have interpreted that there is an annual flux of these 100-ton objects into Earth's upper atmosphere of ten million per year. None of these reaches Earth's surface, but the theory fits well as an explanation for the source of ocean water. This subject will be discussed in Part IV of this book.

The Cometary Flux

Such is the meager comet impact record. A current U.S. Geological Survey program on the asteroid and comet flux in the neighborhood of Earth under the direction of Eugene Shoemaker has much more to work with. A useful system available to

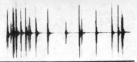

Shoemaker is the cratering flux on Mars, Moon, and Mercury, where erosion interferes minimally with crater preservation. The cratering flux on those stony planetary bodies has been determined with great accuracy, especially for small comets and meteorites.

The second important system for determining asteroid and comet flux is in the active astronomical sighting record. This record is extensive and growing rapidly. Shoemaker's most recent publication finds a flux of about 1,100 asteroids that cross Earth's orbit out of a total comet/asteroid flux of four times that number. This awesome 4,400-body flux is believed to have resulted in nearly 1,500 craters in excess of 10 km in diameter on Earth's land surface during its history, 180 of them greater than 30 km in diameter.

Shoemaker regards his figures as conservative, low, that is to say, as new sightings are still being made and there is much likelihood that many are being missed.

Let us now look at the cataform features developed by cataclysmic impact of an "Apollo asteroid," as these Earth-orbit crossing asteroids are called.

RIES CRATER

The Ries crater, Germany, is perhaps the most thoroughly studied of the larger impact craters on Earth. The feature is securely dated at 15 million years by its sedimentary infill of Miocene lake beds. The 24-km-diameter circular crater is rimmed by a 200-metre ridge of up-turned Mesozoic strata. A *glass lake* underlies the 20-metre Miocene infill.

Several markedly different ejecta types are found broadcast outward from the impact center ("IC") in gigantic splash patterns. A wealth of information on impact phenomena has been gained from analysis of this once-airborne ejecta and from drilling the melted rock represented by the glass lake and the fractured bedrock beneath the crater bowl.

The event, as reconstructed by Von Engelhardt, Pohl, and others (1987), could have been produced by a one-kilometre meteorite travelling at 25 km/sec. Penetrating entirely through a

600-metre thickness of sedimentary rock, the bolide dissipated most of its energy in the underlying crystalline basement. All rock was vaporized down to 2.3 km. A re-frozen melt zone succeeds that to 2.5 km followed by a partially melted zone with both high temperature silica minerals, coesite and stishovite, and other shocked minerals to 4.0-km depth.

Heat generated from the kinetic energy of impact caused rock vaporization. That resulted in volcanic rejection of the vaporized impactor along with much of the impacted country rock. The explosion carried a "mega-breccia" of large blocks of rock, mainly unmelted material from the sedimentary cover. These were broadcast, to 15 km from the IC. Smaller fragments were carried to about 42 km. Following the unmelted, mechanically excavated breccia came a mixture of melted rock, glass, unmelted rock and bombs made up of all of these components. This agglomeration accumulated in a thick blanket over the mega-breccia and adjoining terrain. It has been given the name, "suevite". Suevite is found as much as 25 km from the IC.

The Ries crater's raised bedrock rim is a cataform about 200 metres in height that is topped with fallback breccias. The crater floor, after ejection of the suevite volatiles, was 23 km in diameter. The resultant basin, as mentioned, is today covered with 20 m or less of Miocene and later lake sediments. Beneath them the glass lake of congealed suevite deeply penetrates into the fractured basement rock.

The farthest material ejected from Ries was black rock glass. This material congealed during its trajectory as pellets, which fell in a broadcast pattern known generically as a "tektite strewnfield". The specific tektites believed related to the Ries crater are known as the "Moldavites" and their distribution as the "Moldavite strewnfield" because of its orientation to the eastern European province of Moldavia.

The shower of glassy pellets far southeast from the Ries IC in Moldavia and Bohemia had long puzzled geologists both as to its source but also on chemical grounds. The mineral makeup, according to Von Englehardt (1987) must have been generated by *"selective mineral differentiation within the fluid matrix of the Ries ejecta plume at 10 000° Centigrade"*. This process, astonishing and

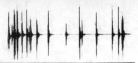

unprecedented in our earthly experience, aptly illustrates one hyper-energy phenomenon that must be considered recurrent among the violent impacts on Earth.

In addition to its mega-features, the Ries cataform has associated micro-features. Shattercones, defined as impacted rock exhibiting conically radiating fractures, are one such manifestation. Impactite minerals such as the previously mentioned very high-temperature forms of silica, coesite, and stishevite are another. Ries crater is a model astrobleme of medium size.

Tektite Strewnfields

Moldavites mentioned as products of the Ries cataform comprise one of the world's four known tektite "strewnfields." These are in order of increasing age [in millions of years, "my"], the "Australasian" (0.7 my), the "Ivory Coast" (1.0 my), the "Moldavian" (15 my), and the "North American" (34 my).

Tektites are known for their dark glassy character and for shapes indicative of congealment during flight. Teardrop and "windswept" looks show the forms imposed by atmospheric ablation as they solidified in flight. Shapes regarded as appropriate for splash debris led to the idea that tektites are products of lunar impact. However, two of the strewnfields are now firmly linked to specific craters, the Moldavian, as mentioned, originated at the Ries crater, and the Ivory Coast strewnfield, which is an impact product of the west African Bosumtwi crater. Two other strewnfields, the North American and Australasian, are without an identified source.

The Australasian, Ivory Coast and North American fields are calculated to comprise 100 million, 20 million and one billion metric tonnes of glass respectively (Glass, 1987). No estimate is available for the Moldavites. I will identify a possible source for the North American tektites later in the book (see Caribou boulders, Part II and Part III).

Siljan Ring

It would be an oversight to discuss astroblemes without mentioning the Siljan crater of Northern Sweden. This interesting impact crater seeps petroleum that must originate in its crystalline terrane, an occurrence that most geologists reject as impossible.

These oil seeps and the drilling of the Siljan ring are not on the subject matter of this book, but the retention and release of volatiles from mantle depth very much is on the subject. It will come up in the pages ahead.

Gastroblemes

Notwithstanding the high level of public and scientific interest in astroblemes and impactor fluxes, serious attention to gastrobleme cataforms and their origins has lagged. Volcanicity of everyday varieties is more readily studied than the rarer deep-source mega-volcanic "events" that result in gastroblemes.

The idea that such features even exist is not generally understood or accepted. Scientific recognition is lagging for volcanos that do not eject volcanic rock, vents which have conducted gas and water but no molten rock from mantle depth to surface. The mechanism allowing emplacement of breccia pipes and kimberlites is involved but little understood. These are the burning issues that need to be considered to advance understanding of gastroblemes.

By their lack of characteristic effusive rock, gastroblemes are less recognizable than normal volcanos. The work of Rice on mantle chamber explosions in the wake of the Mt. St. Helen's eruption and that of Gold in connection with the Siljan Ring and kimberlites have suggested systematics for the release of mantle volatiles. That such releases can occur at all from mantle depths must be a prime concern of anyone interested in crater analysis.

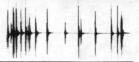

Mantle Chamber Explosions

The question we must ask now is what difference there is between a crater relict after a meteoritic asteroid or cometary impact, an "event" of exogeny, and that left by mantle chamber explosion, an "event" of endogeny? What visible record supports an *endogenic* interpretation over its counterpart?

Firstly, there is controversy in the geological literature disputing the origins of many specific craters and circular features. The term "cryptoexplosive structures" is commonly employed to express the generic description encompassing either type without bias. Vredefort itself, the largest astrobleme listed by Grieve and Robertson and the cataform for which Dietz in his epochal 1961 paper coined the term, is regarded by many geologists as endogenous rather than exogenous. More on this later.

Meteor Crater

Controversy has been frequent on the subject of crater origins. especially as to the larger craters, but also the smaller ones. A prize example is Meteor Crater, Arizona. From the earliest day, when G.K. Gilbert, the renowned geologist of the U.S. Geological Survey (whose legendary work in connection with Lake Bonneville will receive attention later in this book), came on the scene, dispute has ensued.

Meteor Crater was discovered in 1891. The dimensions of the feature (USGS source) include 1170-1205 m internal diameter, lake deposits on the floor 23 m in thickness, their top being 125 m below the desert surface, and a crater rim 40-50 m above that surface. The host sedimentary sandstones and limestones slope up at about 10° toward the crater and then in the rim to 80°. Ejecta is strewn beyond the rim with blocks weighing up to 3 600 tonnes nearby and smaller debris as much as four km distant.

Twenty tonnes or so of nickeliferous iron have been collected from the crater floor and the ejecta blanket around the feature. This provided a reasonable basis for believing that an iron meteorite had slammed into the flat desert floor. At least, that seemed so to the local people at the time.

Such did not persuade the government geologist sent out to investigate the feature, however. After study, G.K. Gilbert pronounced Meteor Crater volcanic. Everyone now agrees that he was mistaken. But the matter was not generally agreed until seventy years later, when the space program demonstrated the ubiquity of impact on the rocky bodies of the Solar System. That Gilbert's "expert opinion" was wrong all along while common sense opinion was right should be encouraging to others with "contrarian" views.

Curiously, the peripatetic Gilbert in 1890 declared lunar craters to be impact features, not volcanic. His prescience has proven right in this case for the most part. Lunar craters *are* largely impact features, although in the case of the very large ones, volcanism is thought to have released lavas that congealed as the "mare" infills.

Notwithstanding the consensus after one hundred years as to the nature of a simple feature such as Meteor Crater, there is little consensus as to the origins of many larger crater-form features. Vredefort, South Africa, and Sudbury, Canada are such forms where dispute persists.

Origin of Columbia Flood Basalts

Alt, Sears, and Hyndman (1988) advanced the idea that large impact craters, which are scantily represented on Earth, must nevertheless have been formed with the same frequency as on the Moon. They then went on to point out that obvious candidates for undiscovered impact sites are the flood basalt plateaus, of which the Columbia is one, the Deccan flows of India another, and the Karoo of southern Africa a third member. These are Earth's most prominent flood basalts.

Using the Indian Deccan flows, the largest on Earth as the prime example, Alt et al propose that impacting released molten mantle magma through the shattered crater roots to form the Deccan flood basalt. Another effect, they think was plate movement: the Seychelle Islands starting as the southwestern rim of the K/T-aged impact crater, drifted 3 000 km southwestward from the Deccan feature. No breccia blankets or glass are reported to substantiate impact.

Turning next to the Columbia plateau, Alt et al propose that dike swarms and faults radiating north and northwest from southeast Oregon are convergent there with the southwest-northeast-trending depression of the Snake River Plain. This implies a southeast Oregon impact site. They surmise that the Miocene basalt eruptions mainly emerged from fissures situated 200 km to the northeast of the impact center.

The Columbia flood basalts are the smallest of the aforesaid three flood basalt terranes. The Karoo and Deccan are larger. None of them has an apparent crater form nor any other sign of astrobleme origin unless one can be convinced of the spreading center interpretation for the Deccan/Seychelles topology.

The Columbia plateau extrusion "event" of late Miocene age (16-17 my) spread basaltic lava over 100 000-200 000 km² of eastern Washington and parts of adjacent Oregon, Idaho, and British Columbia. The idea that a large impact triggered the release of these plateau basalts leads to some problems, however.

Alt and Hyndman do not explain why the Columbia "event" did not lead to plate separation as the Deccan occurrence did. Neither do they offer any help in locating ejecta, which should have been produced as it was in the case of Ries crater, a lesser feature of about the same age. Indeed, the extensive volcanic cover of the environs of the supposed impact site can be invoked as an impedence to finding of ejecta. But nevertheless, some of it should be prominent.

For these and, perhaps, other reasons, the geological profession has not jumped to accept the Alt theory.

THE "K/T EVENT"

The "cause célèbre" for the last ten years in hyper-energy geologic news has been the theory of Alvarez et al (1980) of a meteorite strike that decimated the Earth's biota and yielded an iridium-rich aerosol at the Cretaceous/Tertiary boundary. This idea has been a centerpiece of conferences, the latest of which was the Lunar & Planetary Institute's Snowbird II meeting of October, 1988. Clark R. Chapman reviewed proceedings (EOS, 4/4/89), using expressions such as "...impact [initiation] of the K-T extinctions was strongly supported" and "the debate is now mainly over." Alan Rice, another participant, corrected him, pointing out that perhaps 30% of scientists disagree (Science 2/17/89) and regard endogeny as the likely cause of boundary clay phenomena and associated biotic attrition. I was there and count as one of the 30%.

It is illustrative of the high caliber of scientific information that is being developed in this field to quote from an abstract by Gerta Keller (EOS, 4/18/89). Studying major extinction events close to the K/T boundary in the Brasoz River section, Texas, this researcher finds *two* such extinction events. She says:

"The first extinction episode with 46% of species extinct occurs at a...unit interpreted...to represent a tsunami bed generated by the K/T bolide...[This occurs]...17-20 cm [stratigraphically] below the K/T boundary... The second extinction phase with 45% of species extinct occurs 25 cm above the K/T boundary... No species extinctions or major faunal assemblage changes are directly associated with the K/T boundary. Iridium is ambiguous, with one peak in the upper part of the tsunami bed and a second peak at the micropaleontologically defined K/T boundary.

Magnetostratigraphy indicates that the first extinction phase began about 310,000 years before the K/T boundary and the second...about 50,000 years after... The hypothesis of a global catastrophic mass extinction at the K/T boundary caused by a large extraterrestrial impact is not supported..."

Those closing words, "not supported", are an understatement. The averred findings deny the possibility of impact extinction by a

single impactor at the instant of time known as the K/T boundary. The process proposed by Alvarez cannot be met under Keller's conditions. Two impacts 360,000 years apart are still a possible partial explanation. But impacts in any number do not make good explanations for faunal extinctions spread over a 400,000-year interval and tens of thousands of years from each other.

The Keller study is but one of many produced in the ten years since the Alvarez theory was published, that clearly reveals the serious temporal misfit between the instantaneous iridium aerosol and the extinction record. Her study negates the correlation; and it supports instead the idea of worldwide endogeny with volcanism over 300,000-400,000 years, the Deccan flows being the largest of them.

Mantle chamber explosion can be considered the source of aerosol components, both the siderophile iridium and its companion, shocked quartz. Iridium specifically is produced as a gaseous flouride from Piton de la Fournaise, a volcano related to the Deccan basalts. The quantitative emissions could have provided the aerosol of the K/T boundary clay (Toutain & Meyer, 1989).

Astro vs Gastro, the Dilemma

The geologist may not be able to determine at a glance whether a particular structure is exogenic, endogenic, or a composite. An impactor moving at speeds of 10 000 - 80 000 km/sec can shatter everything down to and including the upper mantle. Its kinetic energy converted to heat vaporizes the impactor and the host terrain in the immediate neighborhood. The vaporized projectile and proximal country rock then explode back from the crater; and high-pressured volatiles may be released through the impact shatter-front. Thus, it may be difficult to distinguish products of rejection after impact from the mantle mineral products released from a high-pressure mantle chamber explosion as a consequence of impact.

Conflicting evidence favoring exogeny or endogeny on much-studied crater features such as Vredefort, South Africa, and

Sudbury, Canada, may result from combination origins. Exogeny that triggers endogeny would be expected to produce complex petrology.

In the case of an "iron meteorite" the geochemical association of metals is said to be siderophile, meaning literally, moon-loving. The grouping of metals is out of place on the crust of the Earth, but may occur in the Mantle or in "oceanic crust", which is thought to be extruded from the Mantle and, hence, to be of "mantle type". This type is known as "ultramafic", that is, made up of the heavy silicates of nickel, iron and magnesium.

Ultramafic magmas, the molten rock that floods upward from the Mantle, or the diapiric plugs of solid rock that are squeezed upward, rupturing their way through shallower cover rocks, are sources of new crust of oceanic- or mantle-type.

The emplacement of new magmatic bodies at depth and the breaking out on the surface of new diapirs in this fashion is an ongoing process today as well as a prominent factor in historical geology. These processes happen at locations known as "spreading centers", places the existing Crust has parted to allow entry of newly-arriving material from below. Spreading centers are most often, but not always, in ocean basins. This is in part because oceans occupy three-quarters of Earth's surface. But the main reason is that the Crust under the oceans is thinner than on the continents.

Ultramafic geochemistry characteristizes the asteroids and comet cores. The affinity of iron and nickel with the platinum group elements includes the latter as "siderophile metals", which can be expected to occur preferentially in ultramafic terranes.

Taking the Alvarez proposal on which so much effort worldwide has been expended, definitive exogenic origin is not yet certain. The original proposal favoring exogeny was predicated on the anomalous siderophile iridium metal in the thin K/T boundary clay proving an asteroidal origin. On the basis of geochemistry that I will present in the pages ahead and the evidence of Toutain & Meyer, it is my view that this deduction is not justified. Endogeny is very much a possible explanation of the K/T "event".

Even where an impacted terrane has a distinctive sedimentary

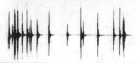

cover with levels of markedly different rock type and sorting out of the components of ejection seems clear enough, if there is no clear evidence of foreign bolide matter (as there is not at the Ries crater), resolution of endogeny versus exogeny can still be elusive. Further complicating factors can be post-cataform volcanism or sedimentation, either of which may mask earlier features.

Thus, the finding of an indisputably endogenic cryptovolcanic structure is not necessarily simple. I know of only one such cryptovolcano that *is* indisputably endogenic, Gros Brukkaros, Namibia.

GROS BRUKKAROS

QUINTESSENTIAL GASTROBLEME

The Gros Brukkaros structure, Southwest Africa (Namibia), is the best example of indisputable endogeny known to me. As a caldera that never ejected any volcanic rock, this magnificent structure, bursting from the crest of a great welt on the ancient shield pan-plain of southern African desert, commends itself as the quintessential gastrobleme. Dimensions of the structure and a conducted tour were provided me by Dr. Roy Miller, Director, Geological Survey of Southwest Africa (now Namibia).

The welt from which the Gros Brukkaros caldera erupts is 7.5 km in diameter; the crater itself is circular and 3 km across. The swell on the flat Namibian desert rises 230 metres; the crater walls rise a further 370 metres.

Cambrian quartzites comprise the surface of the welt and mainly dip gently away from the crater, the bevelled edges of the beds testifying to a greater height before erosional bevelling of the former upper elevations.

The steep crater walls are composed of highly indurated mudstones (the "Brukkaros sediments"). Immediately adjacent to the mudstone walls outside the crater Cambrian quartzites dip as steeply as 26° inward toward the crater. Beneath the crater lip of mudstones are local remnants of younger Cambrian shales, which have been shielded from erosion by the crater walls.

SCENE *1*

GROS BRUKKAROS GASTROBLEME

Above: The crater and welt from a distance; note canyon at center of rim.

Right: Southwest exterior flank of crater.

Below: Canyon breaching crater rim in background, view from the site of a radial dike.

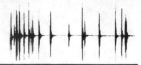

SCENE 1

GROSS BRUKKAROS GASTROBLEME

Above: Inside crater, primitive tree with paper-like bark covering a bundle of fibers (no woody trunk apparent).

Below: The canyon breaching the crater rim.

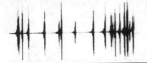

The Brukkaros sediments of the crater rim and walls comprise indurated lake clastics, mainly mudstone as mentioned, but also conglomerates and sandstones. Bedding dips in these strata are steeply into the crater for the most part, the only exception observed by the writer being a drag fold exposed by erosion on the wall of the outlet canyon.

The outlet canyon is a breach 500 metres deep transecting the otherwise continuous, nearly-circular crater rim. The canyon exposes a full section of Brukkaros clastics including the aforesaid drag fold, which testifies to thrust motion *from the crater outward*.

The creation of the canyon itself mandates a lengthy period of water flowing from the crater. Either a pluvial or subterranean water source would have been necessary.

Conglomerates of the Brukkaros sedimentary beds incorporate fragments of rock plucked by explosive volcanism from conduit walls. Because the conduit traverses a well-understood sequence of crystalline basement rocks of the African shield, the origins of some fragments are clearly identifiable.

In addition to the recognized conglomerate clasts from underlying wall rocks, Brukkaros clastics contain a highly important contribution of Permian Karoo shale fragments. These provide critical evidence for interpreting the crater history.

Karoo shale originated as freshwater clay laid down in lakes amid glaciers. Boulders dropped into the clay matrix from melting ice rafts provide evidence for nearby glaciation. The Karoo shale component of Brukkaros conglomerates cannot have come from below the volcano, because none of it occurs there.

Neither could a Karoo deposit over the volcano site before eruption have provided this component. If the original explosive event creating the crater had burst through a Karoo cover, it is unlikely to have by-passed any Karoo material situated within the crater perimeter. Instead, the violent explosion would have excluded Karoo rock from the immediate area; and none would have collapsed back into the caldera.

For Karoo clasts to become incorporated in the muds of the Brukkaros caldera, they would of necessity have originally been deposited *in a pre-existing crater which then was reactivated as a surging mud volcano*. The original explosive event, then, must

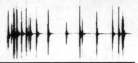

have occurred before Permian Karoo time, whereas Brukkaros sedimentation developed from post-Permian mudflow events.

The drag fold in Brukkaros strata shows that after initial caldera collapse, renewed emission must have occurred so that the Brukkaros sediments carrying the Karoo clasts that had sagged back into the caldera, could then be thrust upward and laterally from the caldera. Successive cycles of this collapse and ejection are implied between Permian and middle Cretaceous times.

In later Cretaceous time a carbonatite dike was emplaced on the south flank of the Gros Brukkaros welt. Its 84-million-year age is the only radiometric date available for the structure. Other dikes were emplaced around the vent in this period, but in what order is not known. Variously these have other petrologies that include peridotite, lamprophyre, and kimberlite. The kimberlite dikes in particular, but also peridotite, carbonatite, and lamprophyres, are recognized as Mantle derivatives.

Clasts of Gros Brukkaros sediments, surficial in origin, have been found in one of the kimberlites. This indicates that Brukkaros sediments were deeply ingested *down the conduit*. Occurring in the same terrane as the kimberlites, the several dike types imply discontinuous magmatic intrusion interrupted by repeated sealing off of emission vents. Each later intrusive was forced to open a new conduit.

Because the Brukkaros sedimentary rock is highly indurated with silica, it is likely the vent sealing process that occurred after each dike system was emplaced was one of silicification. These dike emplacements are situated radially around the caldera on the flanks of the welt. They were explosive events, especially the Kimberlites, bursting through the roof of the swell.

From the foregoing data we can interpret a clear order of how the Gros Brukkaros structure developed. It is as follows:

1. Original crater: Explosive gas cratering in post-Cambrian/*pre-Permian time.* The surface around the crater must have remained low or been peneplaned by Permian time in order that Karoo sediment could be deposited across the conduit mouth.

2. Mud and water volcanism with Brokkaros sedimentation in post-Permian/pre-late-Cretaceous time. Surging emission of mud and water alternated with periods of crater collapse in this

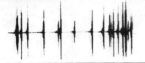

period. Mudstone deposits in the crater were followed by crater collapse and the mudstones falling into the conduit, only to be regurgitated and pushed out upon the bevelled Cambrian apron of the welt.

The collapse process was sufficient to take some Brukkaros material deep down the throat, whence it was positioned to be sealed off, later to be picked up by explodimg kimberlite debris.

The welt that we see today expressed in bevelled Cambrian quartzites as well as the crater rim and flanks constructed of Brukkaros sedimentary rocks, took its form in this period.

3. Dike events in Cretaceous time: Low relief at this time implies that the crater was inactive, likely plugged by silica deposition, thus setting the stage for diversion to the flanks of the structure of the successive intrusive events represented by the dikes.

4. Latest volatile event, Cretaceous/Tertiary: comprised welt dilation and massive emission of liquids and gasses through an enormous crater opening. Sediment from the flows, deposited repeatedly in the crater, was pushed out by renewed emission, thusly building high crater walls. A deep canyon breaching the crater rim accommodated effluent water. Rainfall may have supplemented subsurface water sources but seems unlikely to have been alone sufficient to excavate the canyon.

The great age of this astonishing structure, 300-500 million years, is hardly less astonishing than its apparent conduit to the Mantle. Mantle-type rock has moved up the conduit. At times surface rock has moved down in the vertical corridor. Magmatic intrusives have proceeded from mantle depths in this duct. Copious water and mud effluence has led to the formation of the Brukkaros strata. And high-velocity gas with entrained rock has emplaced kimberlites. Clearly mantle chamber explosion is involved. The provenance of the water and gas is less clear, since none is available for our examination.

Between each "event" of the long-lived gastrobleme, its throat was plugged by silica. The situatiom today has the earmarks of another period of plugging off.

At no stage has Gros Brukkaros ever produced lavas or pyroclastics characteristic of crustal volcanos, only water, mud,

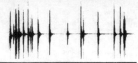
and [probably] enormous volumes of high-pressure gas. The enormity of the events, especially the last one, is underscored by the size of the crater: three km in diameter. What volume and pressure such an orifice would require to maintain its opening at the surface is not so easy to visualize.

Thomas Gold dealt with some of these questions, the kimberlite problem in particular, in his book "Power from the Earth". His discussion is especially germane to the Gros Brukkaros situation, as he deals with the pressure, temperature, and conduit constraints for the occurrence of diamond and its kimberlite host rock.

Kimberlite is an explosion product that has reached the surface from mantle depth (variously 35-3500 km). Expanding volatiles are thought to have supplied energy for the *very high speed* delivery of kimberlite.

Diamonds often occur in kimberlites, and can have only formed under the pressures found at mantle depths. But diamonds, to survive, require reducing conditions and temperature low enough to prevent their combustion. Gold theorizes [and I think correctly] that cooling in transit must have been achieved through gas expansion. Reducing conditions could have been maintained if the gas had been methane, hydrogen, or carbon monoxide. "Obviously," he says, "we are not dealing with the ordinarily known volcanic processes, for they deliver hot magmas at the surface, in which diamond could not survive." (p39).

Thus, we are driven to conclude that **Gros Brukkaros must have erupted methane, hydrogen, carbon monoxide or all of them to have maintained reducing conditions for diamond preservation. The provenance of these gasses and liquids, as with the rock types, must be the Mantle.**

There is another problem, however, which still must be considered: the openness of the conduit. Gold observes [also correctly, I think] that rock pressures would never allow a simple pipe-like conduit to be open from mantle depth to surface for a long eruptive blowout ("Positively, what one cannot have is an open path from a deep source to the surface.").

Gold's resolution of the conduit problem is an ingenious one. He imagines a series of vertically elongate chambers opened

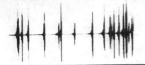

explosively by the eruptive. Each chamber has two vertical pressure gradients. The first is internal hydrostatic pressure, the incremental pressure of the contained water (or whatever fluid is present). The second pressure gradient is lithostatic, the rock pressure in the walls.

It is apparent that descending in any chamber the hydrostatic pressure increases much more slowly than the lithostatic pressure beside it. Thus, at a critical point the chamber walls collapse toward one another, thus establishing the bottom of the chamber.

However, underneath any chamber there are still volatiles in the Crust or Mantle and pressures that cause them to seek lower-pressured environments. When the pressures motivating these deep volatiles exceed lithostatic pressure, they become upwardly mobile, rupture their chamber walls or roof and break into a lower-pressured terrane. A whole series of these chambers will comprise the "conduit" from Mantle to surface for anything making that trip.

From a practical point of view it has long been known that porosity in sedimentary rock closes by plastic flow at depths of 4 000-6 000 m, depending on the rock. At deeper levels rock behaves with greater plasticity, thus suggesting that the differential pressure "cell" height may be less at deeper levels than in the near-surface environment.

One can envision a pulsating action through successively higher chambers, a series of decompression chambers leading from Mantle to surface. Each one would contain a chaotic mass of volatiles and debris temporarily stalled and captured. The migration process in which the chaotic cloud would surge upward in great pulses, one chamber at a time, could proceed over centuries, years, days, or minutes. Each stage would necessarily be the explosive creation of a new chamber upward or outward.

It is interesting to contemplate the present situation at Gros Brukkaros. The vent is apparently plugged with a silica seal, the conduit dormant. This is the same aspect found in middle Cretaceous time before the "events" of explosive dike emplacement. Perhaps today the great welt on the desert overlies a reservoir of steam or methane.

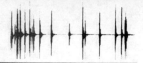

Astro vs Gastro: Discrimination

Having now considered typical impact and endogenous cataforms, the mental images of the reader may be sharpened by a summary of the features geologists look for to differentiate between them.

Gastrobleme character is likely to show doming, a serrate crater rim and somewhat irregular crater shape. Sedimentary strata of pre- and post-explosion terranes may be dipping both into and away from the crater. Mantle minerals, kimberlites, and other basic intrusive rocks figure prominently as dikes and other emplacements at gastrobleme sites. Prominent collapse structures, calderas, and associated minor tectonic structures are to be expected.

Astrobleme character demands circular to oval form. A crater is apt to be rimmed with pre-impact stratified rock turned up steeply or overturned outward (dipping toward the crater). Blocks of the impact host rock are apt to be thrown into distal blankets, which then may be overlain by melt rock that had been thrown higher. A pool of frozen melt rock is apt to occupy the crater center. The country rock below and around the melt rock pool is likely fractured and injected with melt rock and entrained breccia, a lithology known as "pseudotachylite".

The occurrence of shocked rocks (shattercones and pseudotachylite) along with shocked minerals (coesite and stishovite) and multiple planar fracturing on both microscopic and megascopic scales, often in several planar directions, have been thought to prove impact origins. However, recently all of these features have in isolated cases been found far removed from the environs of known impacts. Their diagnostic qualifications for positive impact identifications are, thus, suspect.

The examples given in this chapter of cratering mechanisms and cometary impact are on scales that could be thought of as manageable for study purposes. That is, for each of them a substantial part of the residual cataform evidence can be viewed within one's field of vision at one time. Let us now look at one so

grand in scale that a viewer would require a station in space to see it all. And let us focus on its subtler component circular and hexagonal features, shadow-cataforms, as it were.

ORIGIN OF THE KLAMATH ARC

The Klamath Mountains of northern California and Oregon comprise a veritable macrocosm of the phenomena of endogeny, the accretion of planetary surface by additions of rock from mantle depths. From this statement the knowledgeable reader will be apprised of my viewpoint, which diametrically opposes some elements of prevalent doctrine.

The hypothesis of plate tectonics has been applied in the Klamaths with a broad brush. The whole province is treated as one of "accretion", the translation by a sliding-in mechanism of

MOUNT SHASTA
SCENE 2
Viewed from the Northwest

The present cone is double, Shasta on the left, Shastina to the right of foreground tree. It is this northwest flank that collapsed 380,000 years ago releasing an avalanche of debris that swept fifty km northward.

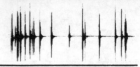

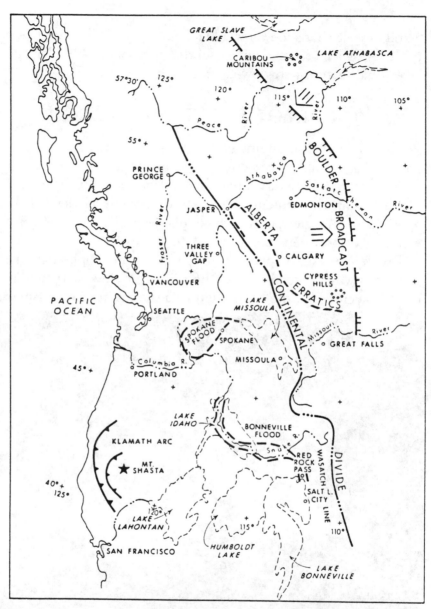

PLATE I

SOUTHWESTERN CANADA
&
NORTHWESTERN U.S.A.

SCALE

0   100 200 300 400 500 km

C. WARREN HUNT   1989

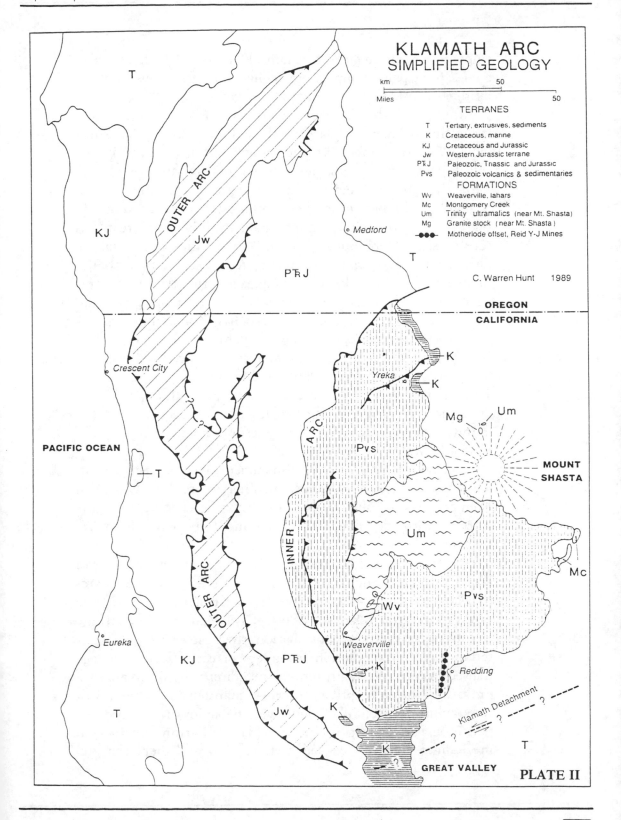

KLAMATH ARC
SIMPLIFIED GEOLOGY

km   50
Miles   50

TERRANES

T   Tertiary, extrusives, sediments
K   Cretaceous, marine
KJ   Cretaceous and Jurassic
Jw   Western Jurassic terrane
PⱦJ   Paleozoic, Triassic and Jurassic
Pvs   Paleozoic volcanics & sedimentaries

FORMATIONS

Wv   Weaverville, lahars
Mc   Montgomery Creek
Um   Trinity ultramafics (near Mt. Shasta)
Mg   Granite stock (near Mt. Shasta)
●●●   Motherlode offset, Reid Y-J Mines

C. Warren Hunt   1989

OREGON
CALIFORNIA

PLATE II

whole terranes from far-distant latitudes (Davis, 1978). This idea comes from paleo-temperature regime interpretations and the latitudes considered appropriate for them.

After arrival, the plate tectonics theory posits the underthrusting of the continental "plate" by the eastward-driving "oceanic" plate. Westward-directed compressional sheet overthrusting is, thusly, motivated by eastward-directed underthrusting.

In this theory elements of the terranes making up the Klamaths, whether lithic elements (sedimentary and volcanic piles and granitic, mafic and ultramafic intrusives) are treated as rootless slabs. "Ophiolite sequences" are mantle-type crystalline ultramafic rock overlain in a recognized sequence by partially-melted transition rock, dike complexes, crust-type rock, volcanics, and sediments. The ultramafics of these igneous piles are thought to form beneath oceanic trenches. Klamath ultramafics have been regarded as dismembered ophiolites, a view broadly supported in the geological community and developed over the last thirty years (Irwin, 1966, Lindsley-Griffen, 1982, Davis, 1966, and many others not listed). Boudier et al (1988) recognize an intact, if somewhat abnormal, ophiolite sequence in the Trinity ultramafic complex, the largest ultramafic terrane in the Klamaths and in North America.

I demur vigorously from the dismembered view and will explain why. Most of the conclusions drawn herein are directly derived from my personal observations after input from astute geologists working with me, Lance W. Pape and (especially) John W. Gabelman.

Examined in the following pages will be the many features of Klamath geology including (1) the multiple mountainous arcs that make up the grand structure (**the "Klamath arc"**), (2) the **100-km sinistral ENE-WSW offset** between the Klamath arc and its former southern continuation, the western Sierra Nevada terrane, (3) sedimentation in valleys of early Cretaceous age incised into the Klamath terrain including massive **lahars of a proto-Mt. Shasta eruptive center,** (4) **mantle rock diapirs,** with ring faulting, "glacierlike" outflowing behavior of extruded serpentinous ultramafic rock, and (5) a **dilation-contraction mechanism that has caused mylonization and diapirism and**

shaped the entire terrane in contrast to overthrusting as the origin of the Klamath low-angle faulting. These phenomena are best explained as consequences of endogeny.

Terranes of the Klamath Mountains

The Klamath Mountains terrane as shown on Maps I and II (reproduced from USGS mapping of Irwin and many others) is readily seen to form subparallel, eastwardly concentric, arcuate belts that are progressively younger westward. This is a much-simplified picture of a series of terranes of plutonic, volcanic, sedimentary, metamorphic and melange complexes that are separated variously by steep and flat faults, or by contacts that may be intrusive or depositional. One may reasonably say that there is something of everything geological in the Klamaths.

Klamath fault style as depicted by Irwin and others follows established styles of Alpine, Appalachian, Canadian Rocky Mountain, and Himalayan overthrusting. Vertical block fault adjustments are seen as superimpositions on prior thrust systems.

The focal point for the multiple concentric arcs of the several "terranes" of the Klamaths (defined by Irwin, 1966) is somewhat east of the present cone of Mt. Shasta, and among basalt flows, vents, and aprons of its late Quaternary ejecta.

Trinity Ultramafic Complex

The southwest edge of the volcanics is just west of Mt. Shasta. It marks the outcrop edge of an enormous expanse of serpentinized basic rocks known as the Trinity ultramafic complex or Trinity peridotite. The serpentine outcrops north of Mt. Shasta as well (Plate II). Fuis (1987), reports that his refraction seismic work reveals a continuation of the Trinity peridotite in the subsurface beneath Mt. Shasta and extending far to the east of it.

The Trinity ultramafic complex, as mentioned, is the largest such body in North America. The 3 500 km² extent of the

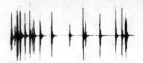

complex west of Mt. Shasta extends in the subsurface under Mt. Shasta and north of it. If the full areal extent is ever known, it may be 10 000 km².

At outcrop the ultramafic body is flanked on three sides by metasedimentary rocks of Paleozoic age. Internally the area of the complex is about fifty percent ultramafic and the other fifty percent gabbros and layered transition units of the former cover rocks. Boudier et al find a steeply dipping west-northwest/east-southeast-striking foliation that *"is related to solid-state flow under asthenospheric [mantle] conditions on the scale of the massif "*. On reaching the transition zone into cover rock the foliation turns to near horizontal. This is *"indicative of partial melting over a magma chamber ... or associated with mantle diapirism"*.

An Ordovician age (435-480 million years) has been obtained for gabbros associated with the peridotite. These are the cover rock ages, the rocks into which the mantle diapirs impacted and were deflected. The youngest rock of the suite, the last arrival, is the peridotite, which may have any younger age. Tertiary age diapirism of the serpentinized Trinity peridotite is recognizable, as I will explain in subsequent pages, and militates against an Ordovician age.

Seismic Response of the Klamath Subsurface

Fuis' analysis of refraction seismic traverses in the Mt. Shasta vicinity, in addition to showing the eastward extension of the ultramafics under the volcanics, also found numerous horizontal sonic discontinuities down to seven-km depth, but *only to the west of Mt. Shasta.* These regional discontinuities cannot be taken to reflect stratigraphy or the tops of horizontal igneous bodies. They are more likely to comprise planes of structural detachment, fault planes, or "décollements" in the traditional terminology.

The Klamath Arc Form

The arcuate form of the successive belts of the Klamath Mountains suggests distortion of previously straight belts, a warp-

ing around a focal point situated east of Mt. Shasta. The dimensions of the Klamath arc are impressive: one hundred thirty degrees (130°) of arc length, a 350-km (220 miles) chord length (north-south), and 170-km (100 miles) radius (east-west, somewhat shortened). In all we see an enormous flexure about a vertical axis.

The term "flexure" implies a bending activity sometime in the past, an intended connotation as the patient reader will see. But before going into origins, first let us describe further the unusual terrane.

Paleontological dating of sedimentary rocks from various parts of the Klamath terrane clearly establishes the prevalence of younger elements toward the west. Ordovician/Silurian on the east gives way to younger Paleozoics then to Triassic and Jurassic westward. A major fault known locally as the "Coast Range" or "South Fork" thrust borders the Klamath "province" on the west, superposing "melanges" and ultramafics above younger marine metasedimentary rocks of the coastal province.

This "Coast Range fault" is treated as a "sole fault" by Irwin and others, I think improperly. This fault has little overthrust character, the emplacement of older rocks over younger. Locally it may even be a low-angle *normal* fault. In reality this fault is better thought of as the outcrop of one of Fuis' décollements.

The origin and nature of melanges associated with the western Jurassic terrane of the Klamaths will be dealt with presently. At this point it is enough to say that the ages of the sedimentary rocks as well as gabbros, granitoids and volcanics are pretty well known, unlike the ultramafic ages, which cannot be determined with present methods of radiometric dating.

Lower Coon Mountain

A peridotite/shale contact occurs at a site that has been studied in detail by the author on Lower Coon Mountain, Del Norte County. This locality is on the extreme western cusp of the Klamath arc just east of Crescent City.

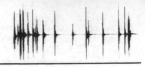

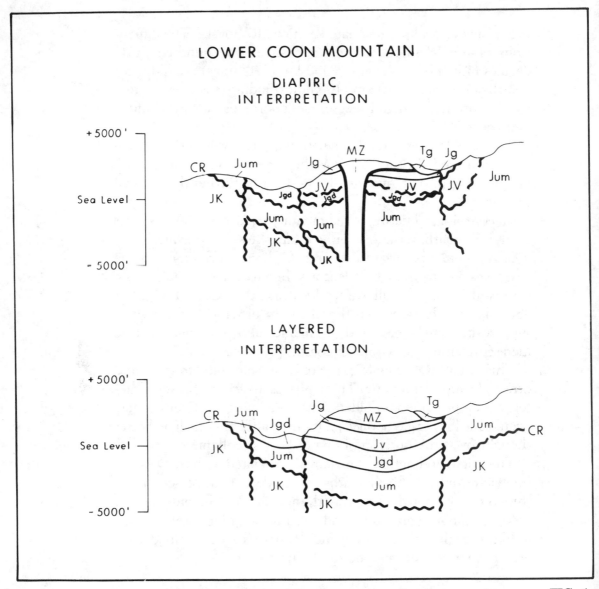

DIAPIRISM VS LAYERED EMPLACEMENT

FIG. 1

Above: Diapiric interpretation of C. Warren Hunt, 1990. *Below:* Layered interpretation after Wagner & Saucedo, 1987.

Legend

Tg	Tertiary gravels	Jg	Gallice fm, slate mainly
MZ	Peridotite, younger	Jv	Volcanics
JK	Metasediments	Jgd	Diorite and gabbro
CR	Coast Range Fault	Jum	Peridotite, older

At that site the profile published with the quadrangle map (Wagner et al, California Div. of Mines, 1987) shows the small ultramafic body as a thin cap on Lower Coon Mountain overlying Gallice slate (Fig. 1). The question of how rock from mantle depth (likely at least 50-200 km) came to the surface is, thus, not addressed by these authors.

Likewise, Norrell et al (1989) have studied the nearby Josephine peridotites, which they group with the Lower Coon Mountain ultramafics. I believe the latter to be younger. Norrell describes the Josephine sequence as harzburgite/dunite overlain by cumulate ultramafic and mafic rocks including gabbro and a dike complex. Above that are pillow lavas, and, finally Galice formation, which includes submarine debris flows (turbidites) and slaty shales (Gallice formation).

The Norrell description defines an ophiolite sequence, which is not replicated at Lower Coon Mountain. There, a gabbro, which may comprise a remnant of breached "cover rocks", does overlie the peridotite. Norrell's upper members are not evident. The peridotite at its edges *overlies Gallice shale and volcanics.* I proved this by drilling a diamond corehole through its eastern edge. In that locality "serpentinite mylonite", as described by Norrell et al in the Josephine ophiolite, rests on horizontally bedded, black, marine, slaty Gallice shale. The sedimentary rock is undisturbed by tectonics or contact metamorphism even within a few centimetres beneath the peridotite. The slaty shale is not fractured; neither is its delicate bedding disturbed in any apparent manner. This suggests marine deposition raised to its present 1 000-m elevation by general terrain dilation without disorientation.

If the Lower Coon Mountain peridotite were a remnant of a dismembered ophiolite sequence, long-distance thrusting inevitably would have disrupted the shale for some distance beneath the fault. This is clearly not the case. **Overthrust fault emplacement of the Lower Coon Mountain peridotite is not indicated.** How then, if there is no disturbance of the slate, could the peridotite have been emplaced?

The truth is not so hard to find. Air photography and thematic mapper imagery clearly show concentric ring fractures prominently encircling the ultramafic pluton (Photo scene 3). Intru-

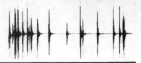

sion of a plug of peridotite (or any rock) creates fissures concentrically around it. Such ring fractures are diagnostic of diapirism. Their prominent expression at Lower Coon Mountain implies that mode of emplacement for its pluton. The drillsite is over one km from the supposed diapiric conduit, far enough that the shale was unaffected by the fluid processes associated with intrusion.

In the process of intrusion peripheral slippage is facilitated if the contact rock is mashed, sheared, and pulverized into the rock type known as mylonite and when groundwater has hydrated its mineralogy to the easily-sheared mineral group known as serpentines. Norrell et al treat this subject extensively in the nearby Josephine ophiolite, where they say *"deformation has acted as a metamorphic process in that it has allowed for the influx of fluids necessary for serpentinization"*. And, *"serpentine mylonites"* occur in *"wide zones throughout the Josephine ophiolite"*.

The slippage planes of the Lower Coon Mountain diapir are not visible because extruded peridotite covers them. Gravitational flowage has taken over the extruded mass allowing it to slump outward from the conduit, especially south and east. In glacial fashion tongues of emergent peridotite, "nappes" in geological parlance, their basal planes turned slippery with serpentinite mylonite, advanced over the adjacent sedimentary and volcanic terrain.

The tongues of Lower Coon Mountain peridotite, in grinding against each other, created wide vertical zones of serpentinite mylonite within the peridotite terrane. These features are much in evidence on the present surface.

The diapiric and out-flowing action is imagined as a slow one with recrystallization accommodating internal shearing. Such is the behavior of salt and ice in glaciers of those crystalline materials. Why might the same not apply to peridotite? The facts at Lower Coon Mountain seem to demand it. Still we must ask, "are these processes necessarily "glacially slow"? On this point the rocks of Lower Coon Mountain are inscrutable.

Misinterpretation of this structure as a thin slab is readily understood because it does, indeed, have flat peripheral contacts and because the conduit is masked under the outwardly-flowing peridotite nappes. Unfortunately, this illusion of flatness engendered the untenable "dismembered ophiolite" theory.

SCENE 3

LOWER COON MOUNTAIN
Thematic mapper imagery, combined bands 2, 4, and 7.
Band 2 is visual green, shown in blue.
Band 4 is near-red, shown in green.
Band 7 is infra-red, shown in red.

The circular pattern overlaid on the lower image is thought to reflect the weathering effects of circular fractures caused by emergence of the peridotite diapir. This likely occurred in late Jurassic time but may be ongoing to some extent.

Hexagons in Diapiric Structures

Hexagons are an interesting manifestation of diapir endogeny, an unexplained form often observed in nature.

Paul Davies in "The Cosmic Blueprint" (1988), explains a similar and possibly related phenomenon. In his words "Bernard Instability" occurs when a horizontal layer of fluid is heated from below, as in meteorology where sunlight heats the ground, which then heats the air above it. The convecting [fluid] adopts a highly orderly and stable pattern of flow, organizing itself into distinctive rolls, or into *cells with a hexagonal structure.* Thus, an initially homogeneous state gives way to a spatial pattern with distinctive long-range order. Further heating may induce additional transitions, such as the onset of chaos." [Emphasis added].

The structure of Little Red Mountain at the southeastern end of the western Jurassic terrane of the Klamaths is a striking example of an ultramafic diapir cell with a circular concentric system of fractures that has taken on an orderly hexagonal form (photo scene 4). At the center of the geometric figure is a vent through which pumiceous volcanic glass has beem explosively released. Photo scene 5 shows this material. Other petrology on this structure is equally surprising. Native copper and nickel-iron alloy carrying platinum group metals are found with exotic, mantle-type rock such as lamprophyre as well as the normal peridotite. The petrology of a chromitite and native metals segregation is summarized in the captions to Photo scene 6.

Flash Volatility

The phenomenon of flash volatility could provide useful insight to the possibilities of undiscovered processes of mineral and element migration. Dikov (1989) reports discovery that the flash volatility of refractory elements is a process *"of a higher order than anything known in conventionally understood thermodynamics".* For example, *uranium and zirconium were flash-vaporized and transported 4 cm in approximately 10^{-5} secs.*

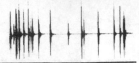

THE BIG HEXAGON   SCENE 4
OF
LITTLE RED MOUNTAIN, TEHAMA COUNTY, CALIFORNIA

A late Jurassic ultramafic diapir has emerged in hexagonal form. Intruding melange of the Permian to Jurassic Rattlesnake Creek sedimentary and volcanic terrane, initial magmatism has been followed by entry and deposition of concentrated platinum group siderophile metals. Explosive emission of pumiceous silica through a central conduit has been the most recent event of this interesting structure.

SCENE 5

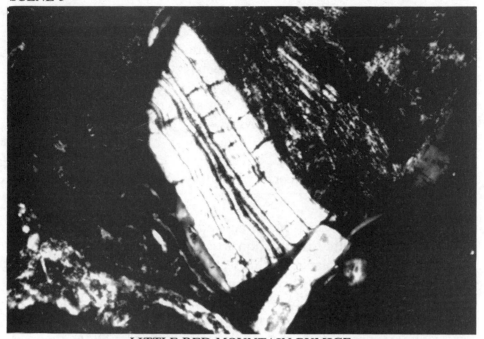

LITTLE RED MOUNTAIN PUMICE
Erupted through peridotite at center of the "Big Hexagon"

Above: Explosively refragmented banded chalcedony and glass. Smaller fragment is muscovite, perhaps a zenocryst from a granite in the conduit (magnified x 150).

Below: Spherical banded chalcedony and glass. The association implies refragmentation after a lapilli origin (magnified x 150).

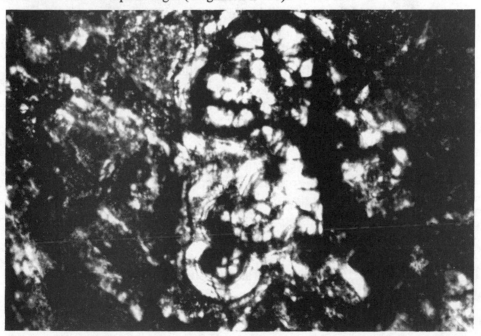

It is not a large step to imagine that this process contains the seed of knowledge necessary to presage the discovery of how migration of refractory elements like the platinum metals can occur. Profound revisions in the science of hyper-energy mobilization and transport of mantle substances to crustal levels could be foreshadowed by this discovery.

Lahars of Proto-Mt. Shasta

If the Lower Coon Mountain and Little Red Mountain peridotites are diapiric, the question arises whether the Trinity complex may also be a diapir. In this section I will describe evidence for Tertiary diapirism of the Trinity complex.

The evidence relies on recognition that a volcanic mudflow, a "lahar", of Eocene or latest Cretaceous age flowed across the now-mountainous outcrop of the Trinity complex. If the theory is true, the mountains must necessarily have risen after the flow.

The story starts with the development of the deep valley system of the Klamath Mountains in early Cretaceous time. South and west of Weaverville these valleys received deposits of marine lower Cretaceous strata, deposition originally continuous with the 40,000-foot "Great Valley sequence". Today only isolated remnants of the valley deposits are preserved.

These valley fills are mainly shales and siltstones, but in places include conglomerate derived from the adjoining hills. They were laid down in straits between island mountains. Their importance to interpretation of the history of the Klamaths is that they clearly show the valleys to have been cut by early Cretaceous time, the age of the sediments.

West and southwest from Weaverville at Hyampom, Hayfork, Big Bear, and Nelson Ranch, deposits of non-marine strata of probable Eocene age comprise clastic and lignitic sedimentary strata up to 700 metres in thickness. They are laid in the same valley system as the Cretaceous strata, of which remnants remain. The preservation of these deposits within the valley system into which Tertiary sediment was deposited leads me to interpret that

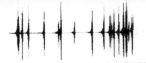
SCENE 6

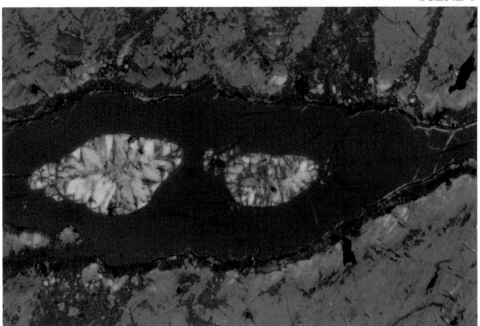

Print 1

LITTLE RED MOUNTAIN
Tehama County, California

Veinlet of asphaltite into serpentine-lined fracture (magnified x60).

Photo micrographs and petrography on these plates by John W. Gabelman.

Print 2

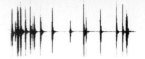

SIDEROPHILE MINERALS
in the
LITTLE RED MOUNTAIN PERIDOTITE

Microphotography and petrography
by John W. Gabelman, description by C. Warren Hunt

Captions for prints number 1 and 2:

Number 1 is viewed under cross-polarized light and magnified x 60. Matrix is serpentinite developed in three stages. Platy antigorite is the main component; and it is being replaced differentially by fine-grained granular fibrous antigorite. The massive, completely amorphous vein filling is interpreted to be asphaltite or anthraxalite. Fibrous antigorite lines the cavity walls and fills the central spaces. Asphaltite has been introduced between two generations of fibrous antigorite, both later than platy antigorite.

Number 2 is the same as number 1 but viewed through a gypsum plate, which serves to verify the fibrous antigorite, platy antigorite and coarse-grained granular fibrous antigorite. The last, which is demonstrated in olivine areas, prevails here. Three serpentinization cycles are represented.

Captions for number 3 and 4:

Host rock is 97% massive, black chromite and picotite without crystal orientation, and 3% pale green-yellow-brown serpentine. The serpentine exhibits vein-like growth and banding with a common orientation within all patches. This orientation is present even where serpentine patches are isolated within chromite-picotite. The serpentine is interstitial to the chromite-picotite and texturally later. The overall rock is rich chromitite-picotite, which had attained a banded state autogenetically before olivine crystallization.

The interpreted history is that chromite and picotite crystals settled as a crystal mush. The porous chromite-picotite mush then was flooded with olivine magma. As the magma cooled and olivine crystallized, volatiles, either from depth or from meteoric waters, hydrated and serpentinized the newly-formed olivine, releasing hydrogen in the process.

The aforesaid volatiles are crucial to deposition of the native metals through migration in organo-metallic complexes (probably as chelates). Their preservation in the oxidizing surface environment may be attributed to reducing environment from this process having continued or, alternatively, to hydrogen permeation from the process of serpentinization of olivine.

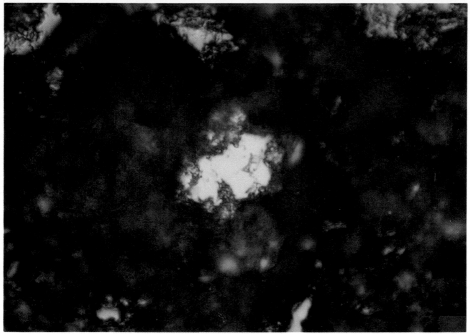

Print 3

LITTLE RED MOUNTAIN PERIDOTITE

Above: Native metals, nickle, iron and platinum, brecciated chromitite in serpentinite matrix (magnified x600).

Below: Platinum metals risidual after 20-minute leach in concentrated HNO_3.

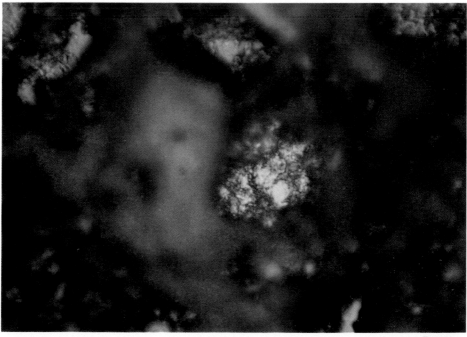

Print 4

It is not known at this time whether hydrogen is still evolving from ongoing serpentinization; and it is not known whether exhalation of methane-rich volatiles from the deep platinum metals sources is still going on. The existence of one or the other of these mechanisms for the maintenance of a reducing environment is required to explain the observed occurrence of native metals in surface rock at Little Red Mountain.

The bright grain in microphoto 3 is admixed iron, nickel and platinum metals. Microphoto 4 shows the same frame after a 20-minute leach with HNO_3. The leaching process has removed iron and nickel (the mineral "awaruite") and left the platinum native metals, as seen in microphoto 4.

Various assays for this rock are as follows:

Metal	Units	USGS	Huntex	Freeport	Cominco
Pt	ppb	1,855*	2,000*	1,600	1,775
Os	ppb		2,000*	4,000	
Ir	ppb	2,415*	1,800*	2,600	
Ru	ppb	2,965*	1,700*	3,100	
Rh	ppb	83*	110*	210	
Pd	ppb	8*	14*	<60	12
Au	ppb		180*	1.5	
Re	ppb		<5		
Cr_2O_5	%		45.01		
Fe_2O_3	%		8.74		
Al_2O_3	%		5.66		
SiO_2	%		9.58		
MgO	%		12.11		
Rb	%		.06		
Sr	%		.01		
W	%		.06		
Ni	ppm	1,545	663		
Cu	ppm	6	12		
Pb	ppm		29		
As	ppm	2			

*Average of two or more assays

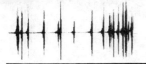

the host terrain has, until perhaps late Pleistocene times, remained at low altitude proximal to sea level.

All these Klamath Tertiary strata were included originally by Hinds (1932) with his Weaverville formation. The main facies of the Weaverville, however, is not lignitic bedded clastics but red volcanic mudflow, "lahar" lithology. Lahar, or debris resembling the product of an avalanche, as Lydon (1969) thought of it, are the only rock types either at Weaverville, the type locality, or northward straddling Trinity Lake. Thus, two wholly incompatible facies have been grouped as Weaverville formation, a mismatch that is still carried on.

The only common features between the Weaverville of the type area and the bedded strata farther west are their common non-marine character and the common topology within the pre-existent, incised Cretaceous valleys of the Klamath Mountains.

Lahar age may not be less than the *oldest* of the "Hyampom" strata, which are in part derived from the mudflow materials. Thus, the lahars themselves are likely of late Cretaceous or Eocene age.

At Weaverville and northward to Trinity Lake the typical non-marine valley-filling Weaverville lahar comprises about 400 metres of loosely consolidated vaguely bedded red mudflow material. In places the formation has a preponderance of locally derived boulder clasts, as Lydon noted. More northeasterly the locally assimilated boulder clasts are less abundant, giving way to soft, poorly-consolidated volcanics of intermediate composition.

Particularly striking in this formation is the habit of boulder clasts large and small to shear flush with the bank in a road cut. (Photo Scene 7) The matrix and clasts have about equal weather resistance, both being semi-consolidated. The sheared clasts originated as fragments of previously deposited volcanics, which were remobilized and tumbled in the advancing mudflow. Fluvially redeposited clasts, by contrast, characteristically have boulder faces that stand out in relief from the bank face, the normal conglomerate appearance.

The Weaverville mudflows of volcanic debris must have flowed 100 km or more to reach their present site, the distance from the

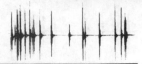

SCENE 7

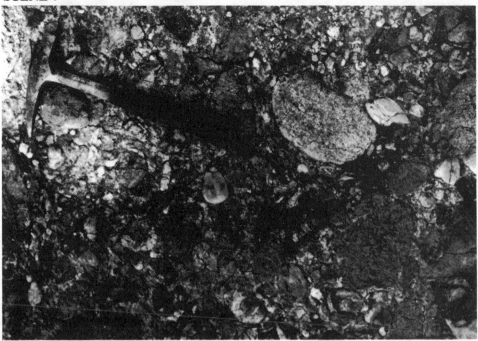

Bouldery lahars of proto-Mt. Shasta: Weaverville and basal Montogomery Creek formations. Note typical shearing of clasts flush with bank. Matrix and boulders have about the same mineral composition, hardness, and resistance to weathering.

present cone of Mt. Shasta. The actual vent may have been farther east. The lahar flow path, thus, traversed the width of the Trinity ultramafic terrain, which must have risen long enough ago to have been eroded to its present serrate aspect. It is fair to conclude from this evidence that serpentinite diapirism of the Trinity ultramafic complex of the Siskiyou Mountains has been 1-2 km since Eocene time.

The proposition that diapirism must have occurred in the last 50 million years does not fit well with the idea of an Ordovician age for the Trinity ultramafics. **The possibility of the quiet existence of mobile, serpentinized ultramafics for 370 to 415 million years from Ordovician to K/T time is inconsistent with their suddenly becoming vigorous in Tertiary times. It is more likely that the Trinity complex was created by diapiric ultramafics in late Cretaceous or early Tertiary time by impacting of a mobilized peridotite mass rising rapidly under and into a previously-existent Ordovician gabbroic cover.**

Returning for the moment to the Weaverville lahars, it is apparent that they should be separated from the lignitic strata farther west. The latter might better be called "Hyampom member" the term Weaverville being reserved for the lahars.

It is a puzzle to me why the very obvious lahar nature of type Weaverville has escaped previous recognition. I would suspect that the lack of an apparent volcanic source, the barrier of Siskiyou mountains, and the 80- to 100-km distance from the nearest possible vent may all have contributed to the mental barrier that has held back recognition so long.

A second occurrence of lahar material of the same age and origin exists, which, likewise, has heretofore escaped recognition. This second deposition is lahar material indistinguishable from that described above. It makes up the basal fifty metres or so of the lower Montgomery Creek formation (Higinbotham, 1987, Aalto, 1988) in roadside outcrops situated southeast of Mt. Shasta and five km or so southwest of the town of Big Bend.

There, the upper mudflow beds of the basal unit of the lower Montgomery Creek intertongue with fluvial conglomerates of the upper unit of the lower Montgomery Creek formation. The upper unit of conglomerates is fluvially reworked lahar material. Where

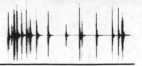

the lahar of the basal unit gives way by interdigitation to overlying fluvial conglomerate, protruding boulders take over from sheared boulders; and precisely visible bedding contacts replace vague and coalescing stratification. Only in the basal unit does one see the clear lahar character.

Higinbotham's attempt to define the age of the non-lahar units of the Montgomery Creek formation led him to a "late Cretaceous to early Tertiary" best estimate of its age. This age is arrived at for the upper Montgomery Creek, which has some fossil content, not for the unfossiliferous lower member.

Thus, we see that the lahars are manifestly a great deal older than the Pleistocene Mt. Shasta volcanics. They must be younger than the marine Cretaceous inliers in the Klamath valleys and the conglomerates that flank the Klamath Mountains orogen. They must be older than the Eocene-age "Hyampom member" that was formerly correlated with them. Those Eocene strata, like the upper unit of the lower Montgomery Creek, are in part reworked lahar material. The Lahars are, consequently, of latest Cretaceous, Paleocene or Eocene age, somewhere in the 70- to 40-million- year bracket.

The basal Montgomery Creek and Weaverville formations, massive lahars on two sides of Mt. Shasta emanated, undoubtedly, from a proto-Mt. Shasta conduit. A crude calculation of volume would suggest a flow containing 600 km³ of rock and an equal water volume. Maximum travel flow distance was not less than 100 km.

It is interesting to compare the Weaverville/Montgomery Creek deposits with a more recent debris flow from Mt. Shasta. Three hundred eighty thousand years ago a debris avalanche from the southwest face of Mt. Shasta swept 45 km³ of debris 50 km northward to cover 676 km² of terrain including the site of the town of Weed and nearly reaching Montague (Crandall, 1989). With about thirteen times the volume and double the travel distance, the Weaverville/Montgomery Creek "event" was at least 26 times as great as Crandall's avalanche. Since much of the evidence of the Weaverville/Montgomery Creek "event" has been lost to erosion, it likely was much greater yet.

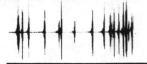

Association of Lahars and K/T Event

We are now in a position to return to the K/T phenomenon and to consider its possible connection with the origin of the Klamath arc. Siderophile iridium in the K/T boundary sediments led to Alvarez' proposal that the "event" consisted of an impact by a 10-km asteroid.

Shock features of distinctive multi-planar and multidirectional character were found in quartz fragments from the world-encircling aerosol that resulted from the impact. Then it was found that the largest quartz fragments occurred in the US Cordillera. This made it appear that the impact site must be nearby in northwestern North America or the adjacent Pacific Ocean basin. A corollary to the quartz particle analysis was discovery of a volcanic surge cloud deposit beneath the shocked quartz in the Cordilleran occurrence. This implied even more strongly that the explosive source must be close. All of this was U.S. Geological Survey work (Bohor et al).

Many programs in other countries have run parallel and produced complicating new information. For example, Graup in Germany and Tredoux et al working on Danish and New Zealand material have indicated a lengthy period for the "event" and numerous metal enrichments. Hansen et al and Gilmour & Guenther have reported widespread soot in the boundary clay. The results of the host of investigators is ambivalent at best as to resolving the endogeny/exogeny question.

In any case, no sufficiently large (80-200 km in diameter) impact crater is present on land to fit the Bohor topological constraint; and none has been found in the ocean. In 1987 at the Cryptoexplosions workshop in South Africa I proposed that endogenic processes at proto-Mt. Shasta could have been the sources for both shocked quartz and the surge cloud. Discounting the attractive position of my proposed source, Bohor insists that only an impact phenomenon can produce the multi-directional planar shock features in quartz that he finds in the boundary deposits. He says that volcanic processes cannot produce multiple

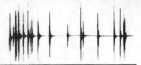

planar shock features. Others disagree; but Bohor's arguments are favored by majority opinion.

The dissenting minority, who favor volcanism as the cause of the K/T "event", point out supporting facts that I find persuasive. These include the following:

1. Multiple "spikes" of anomalous iridium and other metals are found in sediments above and below the K/T boundary horizon. Several metres of sediment thickness is involved, a time interval of 300,000-400,000 years. That spans from the middle of the Maastrichtian stage of the late Cretaceous well into the Danian stage of the Paleocene.

2. Species extinctions mostly do not conform to the precise K/T boundary but are spread over an even longer span of time than the various anomalous metals spikes. Some species were hardly affected, while others were extinguished entirely.

3. Volcanos produce iridium-bearing sublimates capable of introducing the siderophile metals to the boundary clay (Toutain & Meyer, 1989).

This telling minority position is well summarized by A.R. Huffman in a 1989 paper given at NASA's Lunar and Planetary Science Conference. The report concerns the Brazos River, Texas CretaceousTertiary (K/T) section. It concludes that multiple anomalies in various elements lead to the conclusion that "a single instantaneous event is not recorded at the Brazos K/T [but] a gradual transition over 10^3-10^5 years rather than a catastrophic event of short duration."

A similar position was made much earlier by paleontologists, Officer, Hallam, Drake and Devine with the constructive suggestion that worldwide volcanism over a lengthy period better explained the facts than an impact. They suggested the Deccan flood basalts, which have a K/T age, as the most likely site of the endogeny. The iridium-bearing sublimates found by Toutain and Meyer are from the Deccan source area.

Proto-Mt. Shasta may have erupted as part of worldwide volcanism that lasted for a long period and produced aerosols including exotic metals found in the K/T boundary sediments. In any case, its location favors it to be the source of the Cordilleran surge-cloud deposit.

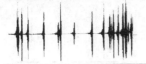

Soot in the Boundary Sediments

Recent reports of the association of soot derived from biomass combustion (wood fires) with anomalous iridium in the K/T boundary clays (Hansen et al, 1987, Gilmour & Guenther, 1988) implies combustion of the world's forest cover as a consequence of the impact or volcanic explosion, which also placed 5 000 km³ of aerosols in the stratosphere. Hydrocarbons and hydrogen of volcanic origin are more likely to have started worldwide fires than the volcanic rejection that follows meteorite impact.

Occurrences of methane in mines in preCambrian crystalline rocks worldwide are abundant and discussed by Gold (1987). Less known is the occurrence of asphaltic petroleum in such terranes. The oil seepage on the Siljan astrobleme in northern Sweden is present in sufficient abundance to have encouraged Swedish interests to attempt the drilling of a nine-km deep exploration hole in search of entrapped liquid hydrocarbons. The well was terminated prematurely for mechanical reasons but not before a significant influx of asphaltic oil had entered its circulating fluid system.

A mantle source of oil in crystalline rocks is undeniably implied by these showings on the large Siljan structure, the fracture system of which penetrates to the base of the crust.

In the case of the Klamath arc, the reader will have noted in the captions of Photo plate 6 that asphaltite occurs in the Little Red Mountain peridotite of the western Jurassic terrane associated with siderophile native metals, chromitite segregations, and a pumiceous explosion breccia. It is not a large step to deduce that a related proto-Mt. Shasta conduit could account for the 5 000 km³ K/T aerosol and the soot component of the boundary clay. Catastrophic release of mantle hydrocarbons from a gastrobleme resembling Gros Brukkaros is an appropriate image.

Mantle Rock Diapirs

The ultramafic intrusive rocks of the Klamath Mountains, which include chromitic dunite, pyroxenite, peridotite, and

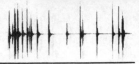

lamprophyres, also carry trace native metals. Copper, iron, nickel, platinum, palladium, iridium, ruthenium, osmium, rhodium, gold, and remarkably, elemental silicon (Bird, 1975). Preservation of some of these in the oxidizing surface environment implies reducing conditions in the rock. There being no alkalinity to the subsurface waters that might provide this, the alternative is a reducing gas, that impregnates the bedrock fractures. Hydrogen or hydrocarbons, are the possible alternatives.

Hydrogen is known to originate with serpentinization, a process that results in magnetite precipitation. Peridotite petrography at Little Red Mountain demonstrates secondary magnetite. Mineral hydrocarbon as shown in petrographic Photo Scene 6, frames # 1 and # 2, could be an end product of the bacterial dehydrogenation of methane. Such dehydrogenation is a common process in the evolution of tar deposits over petroleum seeps. Methane may also have served to facilitate the migration of native metals. It is thought to do that by mobilizing them into organometallic complexes, chelates primarily.

The process of diapirism by which the ultramafics, their volatiles, and the accessory metals rise from mantle depths, is the major characteristic of "spreading centers", where new crust arrives at Earth's surface. The "western Jurassic terrane", which includes both the Lower Coon Mountain and Little Red Mountain peridotite bodies, is a long, narrow spreading center that has been dormant since Jurassic times. In earlier times this narrow north-trending belt may have been a strike-slip shear zone as well as a spreading center in which ultramafic and other igneous intrusives reached the surface from the Mantle.

The other main site of crustal addition in the Klamaths is the Trinity peridotite. This site lacks the elongate pattern of the Western Jurassic terrane and, hence, the implication of an association with strike faulting. Rather, the area of the Trinity complex has a centralized orientation that suggests an underlying mantle plume.

The intrusive activity on the Western Jurassic and Trinity spreading centers is not presently accurately dated, but likely is mainly late Jurassic. In latest Cretaceous or early Tertiary times both the Trinity complex near Mt. Shasta and the Little Red

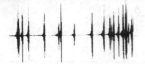

Mountain conduit of the western Jurassic terrane explosively released volatiles, the first on a grand scale, the second on a minute scale by comparison. In Pleistocene times, the Mt. Shasta volcanics forced open the older vents, bursting through the Trinity complex. This renewed activity has built the great cone of the present mountain and spread acidic volcanic ash, lava, and debris aprons that dominate today's scenery.

Any spreading center is by definition a place of lowered pore pressure, a place of extensional tectonics. The reduced pressure regimes allow entry of magmas and diapirs from below, a process that can rupture and disorient the host rock. "Melange" is a term for disoriented and disrupted terrane. "Olistostrome", a stratum of chaotic material produced by seafloor landsliding, is another.

In the western Jurassic terrane melanges of Permian, Triassic and Jurassic sedimentary and volcanic rocks are prominent. The disorientation of the unmetamorphosed melange blocks of the Klamaths has never been explained by any comprehensive theory. Overthrusting, as I pointed out in connection with Lower Coon Mountain, is not sufficient. I suggest that a combination of original seafloor disruption and strike slip shearing followed by a process of dilation and relaxation, as described in the next section, best explains the Klamath melange development.

Terrane Dilation-Relaxation: K/T

Noted in connection with the lahars of proto-Mt. Shasta were Cretaceous and early Tertiary sedimentary deposits in the valleys of the central Klamath Mountains. Down-faulting and tilting are involved in the positioning of these deposits, but the topography on which deposition occurred is substantially preserved. From their original elevations close to sea level, today's sediments have been raised to elevations near 600-700 m. By contrast, the base of the Mt. Shasta volcanic cone is about 1 500 m and the non-serpentine mountain peaks of the Klamaths are near 2 500 m. Relief is on the order of 2 000 m, somewhat more, perhaps, than when Cretaceous and early Tertiary sedimentation was taking place.

While the central Klamaths have risen perhaps from -100 m in Cretaceous time to +100 m in early Tertiary and +700 m now, the Cretaceous Hornbrook formation (north of Mt. Shasta) has risen from, perhaps -100 m to +1 500 m, and the coastal region has risen from -500 m to +1 000 m.

The story is locally much different where the ultramafic diapirs are involved. The mountains of the Trinity peridotite have risen 1 000 to 2 000 m subsequent to the latest Cretaceous or Eocene lahar flows. The emission of the lahar materials implies prior doming of proto-Mt. Shasta and perhaps a great cone such as we have today. Regional dilation must have been followed by an enormous mantle chamber explosion. This sequence provides a possible interpretation of the origin of the Klamath arc, the subject of the next section.

The theme of this section is that quiescence charactertized the Klamaths before the events that resulted in lahar flows and quiessence has characterized them in Tertiary time afterwards despite diapirism of the serpentinite bodies.

Terrane Dilation-Relaxation: J/K

The record of environmental disruption of the Klamath Mountains in the late Jurassic is a very different matter from the relative quiescence of most of Cretaceous and Tertiary times.

Fossil dates of sedimentary elements of the widespread melanges of the western Klamaths span Permian to middle Jurassic ages. Interspersed in the melanges are the younger ultramafic diapirs, plutons of various compositions, and extrusive and intrusive volcanics, some of which penetrate ultramafics. Metamorphism in Permian or Triassic times seems inescapable in the terranes to the east, but is obscure, if present, in the western Jurassic terrane.

To the east of the ultramafics of the western Jurassic terrane, and in apparent superposition on them, the Hayfork sedimentary/volcanic sequence suggests more of the same volcanic/sedimentary sequences but without melange development.

The ultramafics that I have examined in the western Jurassic terrane appear to have intruded as cold diapirs and spread over adjacent surfaces by recrystallization and internal shearing in the manner of glacial ice.

The mechanism of emplacement of mantle-originating ultramafic diapirs that I visualize attributes initial explosive intrusion to the entry of a chaotic slurry of partially-solid, partially-liquid mantle material. The pulse of entry stalls, and further congealing of some phases of the slurry takes place in the conduit. Next, the ultramafic plug is subject to groundwater attack and serpentinization. This causes the plug to be partially converted, especially its peripheries, to less-dense hydrous, and slippery-textured serpentinite. The plug is then susceptible to extrusion upward into lesser-pressured chambers. When it reaches the terrain surface, it may then creep, glacier like, downhill.

The associations of late Jurassic explosive volcanism, ultramafic diapir injection and melange suggest possible simultaneity of origin. I suggest a sequence, as follows: *Dilation of terrain is first. Volcanism is second, an end-point for dilation. Collapse is third. Diapirs are fourth, entering collapse centers as responses to static pressure deficiency.*

Petrologists have long sought an explanation for the "midcrustal melting" that produces migmatites and granitoid magmas. Explosive diapirism, such as I am advocating in the Klamaths, into under-pressured chambers, if followed by solidification of minerals with high crystallization temperatures (olivine, etc.) can release latent heat, which then can liquify host rock to create a granitoid melt. Petrologists Foster and Hyndman (1990) in seeking the source of "voluminous synplutonic mafic magma in the Idaho batholith ... *strongly suggest the importance of subcrustal magma intrusion...to form major batholiths...*" [emphasis mine]. My model should provide the mechanism for midcrustal melting after the intrusion of subcrustal magma. Gold conceived the intrusive process to explain the entry of volatiles and kimberlites. I am extending it as a general process that can involve massive diapirs of ultramafic solids, even as large a mass as represented by the Trinity peridotite complex.

After doming, intrusion and solidification of a peridotite body,

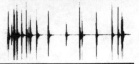
diapirism and the explosive release of volatiles would follow with terrain relaxation. Serpentinization would have caused lubrication of the peripheries during these processes, and movements of the intrusive and its cover rocks at décollements would disrupt the host terrane and create melanges. **Melange development is seen as a mixing during both dilation and relaxation by the slippage of horizontal plates past one another. It is also produced at the peripheries of activated diapirs.**

Crustal addition in the western Jurassic terrane occurred on an elongate alignment. Domes, explosive vents, granitic stocks and ultramafic diapirs along this alignment are frequently marked by peripheral circular fracture patterns such as that shown around Lower Coon Mountain. These show the multiplicity of intrusive events that make up the strike length of the terrane. **This great strike length amply illustrates the overwhelming importance of new crust addition through pressure-deficiency-induced diapirism in creating the Klamath structure in the first place.**

The popular competing idea, subducting oceanic crust as the adjacent cause of Klamath features, is not supported in the field. There is no evidence of rock mass being circulated downward. The assertion of S. Warren Carey that subduction is a myth deserves serious attention.

So much for the combined effect of proximal volcanics, ultramafics and melanges in the western Jurassic terrane of the Klamaths. What can be said about the central and eastern Klamaths and the Mt. Shasta environs? There we find early Cretaceous granite hosted alternately by Trinity ultramafics and Paleozoic metasedimentary series.

The terrane called "eastern Paleozoic" by Irwin includes the serpentinous Trinity ultramafics, which cover more than a 3 500 km² crustal expanse. Various geologists have assigned ages of Ordovician, Permo-Triassic and late Jurassic at one time and another to the complex.

I think, considering that diapirism of the Trinity complex in Tertiary time cut off the flow path used by the K/T (or Eocene) Weaverville lahar, and considering the recurrent explosive volcanism of Mt. Shasta or proto-Mt. Shasta through vents in the ultramafics, the probability is high that similar effusions occurred

as early as the late Jurassic. It is unreasonable with this known behavior as a background to believe that a mobile mass of serpentine could have existed in repose, dormant for the 370-415 million years from Ordovician to Tertiary times. The Trinity ultramafics are likely not older than Jurassic.

Overthrust Terranes of the World

Up to this point specific features of Klamath geology germane to interpretation of its origin have been described. It may be informative to consider what has been deduced by others to explain like situations. Let us look then at the alternative interpretations in the literature for terranes that are understood generally as examples of overthrusting and their relationship to diapirism that imply endogenic crustal accretion.

S. Warren Carey provides interpretations of three such terranes the Alps, Appalachians, and Himalayas. Objecting to the popular understanding of alpine terranes, that is to say, overthrusting as a consequence of horizontal compression [Edouard Suess, 1831-1914], Carey argues for crustal addition at related "spreading centers" as the fundamental cause and origin of lateral overthrusting.

Carey's commentaries on three major overthrust provinces are paraphrased as follows, in his own words where possible:

"THE SURFACE PATTERN OF THE APPALACHIANS is consistent with diapirism but inconsistent with the vice model of compression between converging continents. The front against the miogeosyncline [westward] is bowed into a series of arcs. The overthrusting is most intense where the arcs bow [westward] and much less intense where the arcs bow [eastward] toward the crystalline core. This is what should be expected from a chain of diapirs" [each situated east of a westward bow].

"THE VAN OF THE ALPS are the Helvetic nappes, a stack of flat overthrusts, [which is succeeded to the south by] upturned pre-Alpine basement [and] then a zone of roots and the ophiolites of the Ivrea zone. All this is consistent with the [diapirism] model".

"THE HIMALAYA OROGEN is nearly 400 million years younger than the Appalachian orogen, ... still rising diapirically and thrusting out its nappes [of eugeosynclical sediments] from central Tibet over the miogeosyncline and creating the high Himalaya in the process. The Indus suture, [the spreading center to the north of the High Himalayas, is where] we first find ophiolites and serpentinites, driven up in the rising diapir [the center of which is north still farther.] The ophiolites have been] pushed laterally as a great nappe thrust for 100 km southwestward over the miogeosynclinal strata. The Indus suture [is a sinistral] megashear ... where a whole continent has been displaced [1 000 km] horizontally rather than pushed up and overthrust".

Crust Addition vs Plate Collision

It is not necessary for the purposes here to recap all Carey's arguments in order to consider whether the Klamath province is better explained by ocean crust colliding against the western margin and underriding the continental crust or whether crustal incrementation within the Klamaths and to their east provides a better explanation for observable phenomena. These opposing ideas can be held in abeyance while we look at the evidence.

The first and most obvious condition to explain is, as mentioned, the arc form itself. This form is anathematic to active impacting from the west: "*arc*" form is definitively a product of radiative force from a focal source. Since the arc is concave eastward, the source of energy that bowed it *must* have been to the east.

The second line of evidence is in the problem of melange creation. The melanges are inexplicable by an event of overthrusting or by any other recognized tectonic activity. The idea for melange creation that I have advanced already entails reversing shear motion, the shears being either horizontal or vertical planes. **Horizontal décollements detected seismically by Fuis would seem ideal to accommodate repetitious reversal under regimes of terrane dilation and relaxation. Terrane platelets are imagined as sliding first one way then the other in response to dilatancy and relaxation.**

The third line of evidence is in the topology of coastal stratigraphic elements. If an oceanic plate were impacting the coast, these rocks should be taking the brunt of its force, rotating seaward and buckling under. Observed fact shows youthful (Pliocene) strata along the coastline that are not being turned under. Neither are they apparently fractured by uneven uplift within the hanging wall of a subduction fault surface deep below. In other words, if the Klamath Mountains are being raised by an oceanic "plate" diving below them at the edge of the continental shelf, there is nothing self-evident to prove it on the surface.

Intensity of both metamorphism and tectonic activity is greater in the central and eastern Klamaths than on the coast. The coastline is today emergent and has been advancing seaward since the late Jurassic rather than being buckled under and forced to retreat landward. Subduction theory is not supported by field evidence from the Klamath Mountains.

On the more general problem of the alternatives of compressional tectonism versus intrusive crustal accretion for explaining mountain systems in which multiple décollements are major features [as opposed to monolithic plutonic systems like the Sierra Nevada], one must make an "either-or" choice. The choice is between continental collision between plates detached from their mantle roots *or* diapirism and crustal accretion with nappes thrust outward gravitationally from emergent diapirs. Magmatic intrusions and volcanic exhalations are accommodated by both choices. Repetitious crustal dilation and collapse attended by elevation and depression of pore pressures is only to be expected to be part of the crustal accretion scenario. Inertial tectonism is another aspect of the crustal accretion model that would not be expected to occur with plate tectonic processes.

Inertial Origin of the Klamath Arc

This brings us to a point where we may consider the origin of the arc form in the Klamath Mountains in the context of accreting crust. Collisional tectonism has already been shown as inapplicable because of preserved coastal rock sequences.

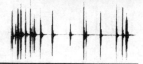

Intrusive mechanics of a rock mass like the Trinity complex would create circular patterns in surrounding rocks and emanating gravitational rock glaciers. But this process would be unable to effect a warping of the enormous outer arc. The deficiency could have been made up by the effects of angular momentum change in the raising of mass from depth. The sudden rise of an enormous mass, whether of solid rock or gaseous, would entail its acceleration to crustal velocity. This would put a westward-directed force on the conduit wall that would increase upward. Rapid injection could move the entire terrane westward, wrenching it loose from its former connections to the north and south. Curiously, the Klamath Mountains are bordered on the south by just such a disconnection, a 100-km left-lateral offset from the Sierra Nevada foothills.

It is interesting that the character of décollement must be attributed to the subsurface discontinuities found by Fuis' refraction seismic analysis in the Mt. Shasta vicinity. These occur only to the west of Mt. Shasta. Thrust faulting in the Klamath terranes is also only known to the west of Mt. Shasta. And, of course, the arc form itself is only to the west. **This assymetry is explainable as the consequence of crustal inertia to the raising of mass from depth. Enormous mass transfer from mantle depth through the Crust must inevitably impose an enormous reaction that retards the angular velocity of the west wall of the conduit.**

This is an instantaneous event in the case of rapid diapiric injection or explosive volcanism; it is a gradual process in the situation where magmatic intrusion and terrain dilation are themselves slow.

A look at some numbers will be instructive as to efficacy of these mechanisms for terrane bowing. Let us consider a mantle chamber explosion sufficiently powerful to raise to the stratosphere an aerosol of 5 000 km³ volume and to lay a 1-cm blanket over the entire Earth. This figure is used because it is the generally accepted figure for the iridium-bearing aerosol that settled on the Earth in the K/T boundary "event".

The expanding gas required to carry the aerosol might have a mass equivalent to perhaps a further 45 000 km³. It would be necessary for us to at least double that so as to take into account ejecta particles too large to stay aloft as aerosol.

We now have 100 000 km³ of ejecta mass, an enormous figure, perhaps unprecedented for airfall material. But then, the K/T "event" *was* unprecedented. By comparison, the great flood basalt flows are in the millions of cubic kilometres. If the mass of the entire Klamath terrane is about thirty times our proposed ejecta mass (60 000 km² x 50 km depth), and if the explosive passage of a slurried mixture moving up from 250-km depth would require it to be speeded up to crustal velocity, a change of velocity of about 31 km/hr, then the reactionary acceleration if applied to conduit walls so as to be distributed radially to the entire Klamath province (an impossibility, but interesting for this analysis), then the whole terrane would have to accept an average westerly velocity of 1 km/hr.

In reality, the force could not have been distributed evenly enough to do that. What would have happened is that the conduit would have been driven deeply into the adjoining terrain in a westward direction. An arc would have formed.

Appalachian Comparison

It is of interest at this point to note Carey's words on the Appalachian situation: "The overthrusting is most intense where the arcs bow [westward]". These words seem appropriate for the Klamath arc also. In addition, it is noteworthy that asymmetry as found in the Klamaths, where the arc is on one side only, is also present in the Appalachians. There, Carey says, large overthrusts occur where arcs bow westward, small overthrusts where the arcs bow eastward. The large overthrusts are opposite centers of added Crust; the lesser overthrusts are between those centers. All these effects are strikingly similar to observed fact in the Klamath Mountains. It is notable that Mt. Shasta is unique among the Cascade volcano chain in having a flanking mountain arc.

Similar features are not present in the Himalayas or Alps because those orogens are situated on cast-west megashears. The sinistral translation found by Carey on the Indus suture of the Himalayan situation may itself be an effect of crustal incrementa-

tion to the north, which caused a 1 000 km westward (sinistral) translation of the north block relative to the south block, another inertial effect. The counterpart in the Klamaths to the translation across the Indus suture is the westward inertial translation of the entire Klamath terrain.

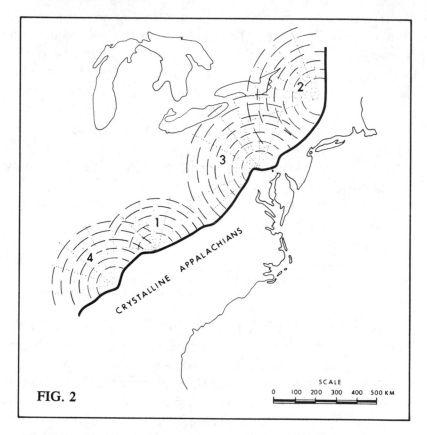

FIG. 2

CRYSTALLINE APPALACHIANS

SCALE
0   100   200   300   400   500 KM

ARCS OF SUCCESSIVE APPALACHIAN OVERTHRUSTING
Interpretation of S. Warren Carey, 1988.

Duality of Klamath Arcs

It is interesting to note at this point that either the raising of mass by explosive volcanism or its introduction to the Crust by impact from space could result in the inertial effects required for terrane warping. A bolide could have triggered incipient mantle

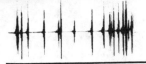

volcanism. There is no evidence, however, other than Bohor's, that one might have done so. The subject is raised because of the possibility that such evidence could later be uncovered.

The Klamath arc on close inspection proves to be a composite of two not quite coincident concentric arcs (Plate II). The smaller *Inner arc* is immediately west of Mt. Shasta and encompasses the Trinity complex. The more distant *Outer arc* has a lesser curvature, and its greater radius of curvature defines the rim of the western Jurassic terrane and the western edge of the Josephine ophiolite on the Oregon-California border 150 km northwest of Mt. Shasta. If emplacement of ultramafic diapirs effects bowing, then the positioning of the two largest ophiolite sequences in the Klamaths is appropriate for that interpretation. The timing of these arc formations would appear to have been late Jurassic.

Detachment Planes

One additional requirement for the creation of arcs is still necessary. The bowed surface terrane must be detached from its roots on one or more horizontal planes. This requirement arises from the fact that different inertial forces result from acceleration requirements at all levels of the ejection conduit. Unless detachment planes occurred, the three-dimensional terrane would have to tilt westward. Unless numerous planes of detachment were present, each plate between planes would itself tilt westward. As we do not recognize such tilting, detachment planes, décollements in traditional parlance, must be present.

Numerous detachment planes would be expected. And, in fact, that is what has been reported as multiple "seismic discontinuities" by Fuis down to seven-km depth. Here then are fundamental Klamath structural features, whether referred to as detachment planes, décollements, or simply as seismic pseudostratigraphy.

Similar décollements are discussed by Charles B. Hunt (1979) in the southern Great Basin, California. The Amargosa fault in the eastern Mojave desert is described by Hunt as "a gravity fault"

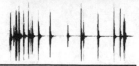

where a 40,000-foot unbroken sequence of preCambrian and Paleozoic rocks has "moved westward onto older [rocks] by gravity sliding".

In northeastern Nevada a similar doctrine is widely believed in connection with the Roberts Mountain overthrust, a fault which cannot be traced on the ground from mountain range to mountain range, but is, nevertheless, attributed with 80-km thrust that emplaced Ordovician "upper plate" strata above younger "lower plate" Paleozoic rocks (Roberts et al, 1971). This is a paleontological interpretation: Strata with "eugeosynclinal" fauna are found above strata carrying "miogeosynclinal" fauna. Hunt comments

> "We can as well assume that the boundary was irregular with limestone banks trending northwest and separated by troughs containing eugeosynclinal sediments. By this hypothesis there would have been several thrusts, each with little displacement as the troughs were squeezed between the resistant banks".

My extensive work in northeastern Nevada confirms C.B. Hunt's interpretation. Long-distance thrusting is quite unnecessary. Repetitious dilatancy and collapse, on the other hand, could produce the "squeezing" without long-distance horizontal compression, thusly better explaining these features.

Other abundantly recognized décollements in the geological literature of the Great Basin are cited by Davis (1979). All of these submit better to interpretation as consequences of dilatancy and collapse than to compressional tectonics.

Pore Fluid Pressure

Elevated pore fluid pressure attendant upon doming and magma entry into the lower reaches of a conduit from mantle depth under conditions of incipient explosion would assist the detachment process and yield multiple décollement planes. Gliding motion on pore-pressured detachment surfaces produces the "flat" overthrusts that are often found in stacks worldwide. The role of pore fluid pressure in producing these phenomena was first recognized and described by Hubbard and Rubey in the early nineteen fifties. It is widely accepted today.

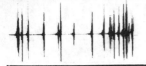

The gliding of a detached terrane above a décollement, while assisted by elevated pore pressure, is also aided by uplift of the thrust source area. The active upper detached plates of the Klamath Mountains would have been much assisted if a proto-Mt. Shasta welt had provided such gravity assistance.

Westward Translation of Klamath Terrane

In addition to its unusual arc form, the Klamath Mountains appear to comprise the westwardly-displaced north end of the Sierra Nevada Motherlode Belt and its flanking terranes. The concept of the Klamaths as a detachment of the northern Sierra Nevada is a natural one for any observant layman and one that is not inconsistent with geology.

There is strong similarity between the age sequences of the metasedimentary and volcanic rocks of the two belts, the rock types appearing to follow through from the one region to the other. The styles of mineralization of the Sierran foothills copper and the Motherlode gold belts are respectively replicated in the West Shasta copper district and the Reid-Yankee John gold trend of the southeastern Klamaths.

A sinistral offset of about 100 km is implied by this correlation. Unfortunately, there is no apparent structural alignment implying such displacement in the surface rocks. It is tempting to try to prolong the east-west-trending Mendocino escarpment from its undersea position immediately west of the south end of the Klamaths to accommodate the apparent displacement. No geophysical or geological alignments across the north end of the Great Valley or through the volcanics south of Mt. Shasta are found that are strong enough to imply continuation of the Mendocino feature across those terranes. Nevertheless, a deep crust or mantle connection cannot be discounted.

It is interesting that the most recent maps issued by the California Division of Mines and Geology (Wagner & Saucedo) depict a westward deflection of the northwest-trending *dextral San Andreas shear* into the Mendocino escarpment. I regard this idea as sterile and incorrect, an impossibility if the inertial origin of the

Klamaths is correct, and contrary to the mechanics of the San Andreas fault, as I will show in coming pages.

Carey's Cordilleran Megashear

S. Warren Carey proposes a dextral distortion of the circum-Pacific megashear, a 100° right (eastward) turn at the north end of the Sierra Nevada. Thence the shear is deflected 500 km eastward where it makes a left turn of 100° and continues northwest approximately in the position of the Rocky Mountain trench. The "Z-form" megashear offset is a drag fold with vertical axes, a consistent feature for the dextral couple.

Carey calls the turn near the Klamaths the "Mendocino orocline" and that in Idaho the "Idaho orocline". It is interesting that melanges of Permian to late Jurassic-age sedimentary and igneous rocks, like those of the western Jurassic terrane of the Klamaths, are exposed in Hell's Canyon on the Snake River in the Idaho-Oregon- Washington border area some 600 km northeast of the Klamaths.

One may fairly ask whether the megashear offset could be the cause of Klamath westward translation or vice versa. Clearly, the sinistral Klamath offset could not result tectonically from the dextral megashear offset. But consider the opposite.

The potential for the whole terrane to have been translated 100 km westward by the inertial process is dependant only on sufficient inertial force, not on anything related to the megashear couple. The fact that the implied Klamath translational motion would be sinistral, contrary to the megashear sense, merely informs us that the translational feature is not something to expect from the regional stress system. On the other hand, **the pressure deficiency engendered by the northwestward convexity from the Mendocino orocline would make Mt. Shasta a preferred place for any sort of conduit to open. The resultant exhalation would cause a net reactive velocity being gained by the Klamath terrane. This would be independent of regional stress and possibly orders of magnitude more powerful.**

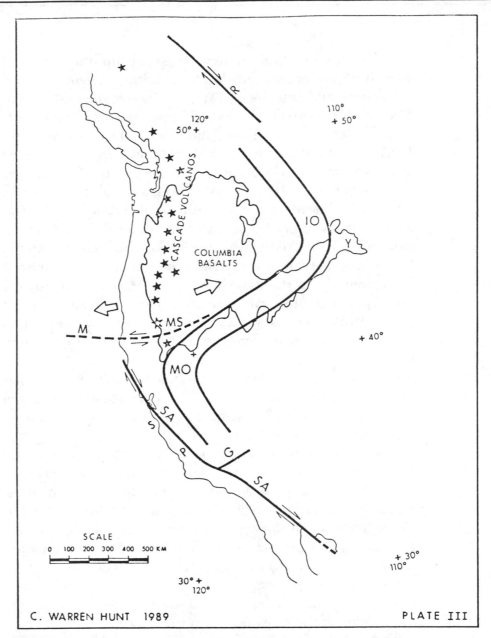

DEFORMATION OF NORTHWESTERN U.S. AND SOUTHWESTERN CANADA
Jurassic to Recent
Adapted from S.Warren Carey by C. Warren Hunt, 1989
Legend

G	Garlock fault	MO	Mendocino orocline	R	Rocky Mountain trench
IO	Idaho orocline	MS	Mount Shasta	S	Santa Cruz
M	Mendocino escarpment	P	Parkfield sector	SA	San Andreas fault

Either the creation of new crust within the aforesaid megashear zone at the proto-Mt. Shasta site or violent explosive volcanism could cause inertial arc formation to the west. Attendant upon this would be a widening of the megashear zone. Eastern elements of the megashear would be offset as Carey envisions. Tensile openings would propagate northwest from the offset allowing the Modoc plateau to the east of Mt. Shasta to separate from the Klamaths, which would be subject to inertial retardation. **The Mendocino fracture would break with sinistral motion. It would *not* become a surrogate for deflected dextral motion of the San Andreas, as current doctrine seems to require. Wrenching motion on the Mendocino fracture has a sinistral sense contrary to the dextral sense of force that created the oroclines. The sinistral wrenching motion is an effect of proto-Mt. Shasta mass ejection. The Cascade volcanos appear to follow a fracture that propagated northward from the ejection site.**

Once started, the inertial separation resulting from crustal intrusions in the Klamaths would be self-perpetuating, the more intrusion, the more tension fracturing to the east resulting in more intrusion, and so forth.

The initiation of all features of the Klamath structure in this scenario is interpreted as consequential upon the bending of the Mendocino orocline. It all would have begun with an initial wiggle in the circum-Pacific megashear. Tension at the Mt. Shasta site allowed diapirism and venting of volatiles through conduits now buried under Quaternary ejecta, and the diapirism and venting would have assisted the orocline bending in return.

Proto-Mt. Shasta explosive or diapiric action and terrain translation could have been simultaneous and complementary to the warping of the megashear into its "Z-form."

The megashear warping event must have preceded Cretaceous sedimentation of the Klamath area as its catastrophic nature would be inconsistent with the preservation of Cretaceous deposits (Hornbrook and others). Even the K/T explosive event, or the ensuing lahar flows would have been orders of magnitude less violent than the Earth spasm of megashear warping and associated diapirism of Trinity ultramafics.

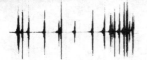

We are impelled to choose the late Jurassic as the most likely time of these violent events and the consequential terrane translation. That was, then, 110-150 myBP, depending on which time scale one chooses.

Summary Interpretation of the Klamath Arc

Whereas the reader should understand that many aspects of Klamath geology are problematical, disputed, and unlikely to be resolved with finality for some time to come, the following generalized activities have produced the present scenery. First, the geological timescale should be kept clearly in mind.

Geological Timescale

AEON	ERA	PERIOD	EPOCH	Years x 10^6 BP
			Holocene	.01
			Pleistocene	2.0
			Pliocene	5.3
			Miocene	24
	CENOZOIC			
			Oligocene	37
			Eocene	54
			Paleocene	85
		CRETACEOUS		
				140
	MESOZOIC	JURASSIC		200
		TRIASSIC		250
PHANEROZOIC				
		PERMIAN		290
		CARBONIFEROUS		360
	PALEOZOIC	DEVONIAN		410
		SILURIAN		440
		ORDOVICIAN		510
		CAMBRIAN		570
PROTEROZOIC				1500
ARCHEOZOIC				3800

Lower Paleozoic: (Cambrian, Ordovician and Silurian time) saw a continental shelf intruded by magmas and breached by volcanic effusions. The gabbroic intrusives of the proto-Mt. Shasta spreading center crystallized at this time.

Upper Paleozoic: (Devonian, Missippian, and Permo-Pennsylvanian time) was characterized by submarine volcanism, clastic wedges, and fringing limestone reefs on the flanks of volcanic islands. Massive sulphide mineralization was associated with the volcanism.

Triassic: continued deposition of fine clastics (shales) and reefal limestones, along with volcanic ash. The Period saw the first granites and intermediate (dioritic) intrusives in the Klamaths.

Jurassic: much increased volcanism pyroclastics, andesitic flows, agglomerates and tuffs, various coarse clastics (conglomerates), and the **first ultramific diapirism in the western Jurassic terranes and at proto-Mt. Shasta. Late in the Period violent uplift, dilation, explosive volcanism, inertial décollements, overthrusting, strike-slip faulting and malange development. Displacement of entire Klamath block 100 km westward. Commencement of entrenchment of present river system.**

Cretaceous: normal erosional conditions with river entrenchment, the order for most of this Period. Approximate present topography established in central and eastern Klamaths. The Great Valley clastic wedge flanks the risen mountainous terrain on the southeast, the Hornbrook formation on the northeast and the South Fork Mountain schist on the west, all of these encroaching on the flanks of the Klamath province and into its flooded valleys. Laterite soils developed on emergent highlands.

K/T transition: probably marked at proto-Mt. Shasta by massive volcanic explosions, pulverized mantle rock with siderophile metals and minerals, steam, and hydrocarbon gas. Worldwide fire storms, darkness, release of lahars, collapse, and renewed ultramafic diapirism especially at the proto-Mt. Shasta spreading center.

Eocene: tropical conditions and continued laterization on high

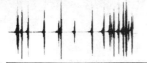

ground, in this period and placer development in the valleys. These are the placers that in subsequent Tertiary time were elevated and left perched high above the incised drainage. Continued incising occurred in the Klamath valleys and caused reworking and redeposition of K/T lahar materials. Reinvigorated diapirism in the Trinity peridotite complex blocked off the former lahar flow path to Weaverville.

Oligocene-Miocene: continued reworking of lahars with lignite and clastic deposition in valleys.

Pliocene: time not represented by fossiliferous sedimentation.

Pleistocene: time marked by renewal of explosive acidic and intermediate volcanic effusion along the eastern edge of the Klamaths. Cone buildup at Mt. Shasta led to at least one massive northwestward-debouching avalanche. This behavioral style continues today.

THE SAN ANDREAS FAULT

In discussion of the Lower Coon Mountain ultramafic diapir the question was asked rhetorically, *"is diapirism glacially slow?"* In this section evidence will be brought out that is supportive of sometime rapid diapirism.

Prevailing Theory: Pacific "Plate" Rotation

The San Andreas fault divides northern from southern California obliquely. Let us first recount the facts known about this fault as well as conventional theories of its cause.

The fault is characterized as a right-lateral, strike-slip fault (opposite side moves to right). The north Pacific basin is thought to rotate counterclockwise, and the west block of the fault to be a part of it. Movement of right-lateral sense is thought to have occurred over some millions of years, and total motion to be upwards of 300 km. Fault motion has been intermittent, stress building up until frictional resistance is overcome. The ensuing

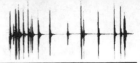

sudden release of energy is, in some cases, devastating. Motion on the San Andreas occurs on "sectors" of the fault, not on the whole fault at once. These summarize the understandings among professionals and public as well concerning the San Andreas fault.

There are some aspects of these tenets that I think require revision. For example, it is quite unsatisfactory to regard the west "block" of the fault as a rigid monolith transmitting horizontal compressional force along its great length, 950 km or more, against a frictionally resisting eastern "block." If that were the case, frictional release on one "sector" would quickly trigger motion on the entire fault length. This clearly does not happen.

The question whether a compressional force can be transmitted by a large expanse of rock is an old one. Hubbert and Rubey (1959, GSA v70, pp115-166) put the question to rest in the minds of most geologists in connection with overthrust mechanisms. They conclusively showed that pore fluid pressure allows gravitational gliding.

Long distance force transmission in a lithic block of the Crust is impossible, because all large blocks of rock are jointed and, hence, incompetent to transmit compression very far. The idea of the San Andreas being under stress just waiting to be released should likewise be put to rest.

If stress were built up all along the fault, the Parkfield sector should have moved after the recent motion on the Santa Cruz sector. For many years now, at Parkfield, there has been a deployment of instrumentation to measure the earthquake expected to relieve the presumed built-up, but unrelieved, strain on that "overdue" sector.

Diapirism: an Alternative Driving Force

Instead of the concept of two earth blocks rubbing past one another, we could treat the **San Andreas fault as an elongate rupture zone transecting the crust. Mantle motions that spread the zone allow volatiles and magmas trapped under the Crust to surge into the under-pressured fractures above them.**

Taking this perspective, let us look at the "Loma Prieta" earthquake (October 17, 1989). Newspapers reported that motion occurred on the "Santa Cruz sector" at 18 km depth. Reports [attributed to Paul Rosenberg of the U.S. Geological Survey] said "massive rock faces on either side of the San Andreas slipped about 1.6 metres past each other, and the west face rode up over the east one. Within ten seconds the rupture had spread roughly 32 km, splitting apart the sides of the fault ... *To seismologists' surprise, land to the west of the fault sprang upward ... The west side has popped up ... and pushed northward ..."* (my emphasis).

McNally et al of C.F. Richter Seismological Laboratory (EOS Nov. 7, 1989) reports motion of 1.7 m right lateral and 1.3 m reverse (west side upward) sense on a fault surface dipping 70° southwest. Focal depth was reported as 18.24 km beneath a point some 6.5 km west of the fault surface trace.

The motion reported should come as a surprise only to someone who was convinced ahead of time that the west side should not be rising but buckling under as subduction drags it under the continent.

I suggest that the motion report should be taken at face value. The epicenter, 18 km deep and 6.5 or so km west of the fault surface trace would suggest a 70° west dip if a plane of slippage were involved. But who can say that such a plane exists to 18 km depth? The deepest hole man has ever drilled is less than one-half that figure, which is notably far beyond the point where plastic flowage in rock occurs. How could there be any buildup or release of frictional stress at 18 km depth? My solution is explosive passage of mantle materials into an under-pressured crustal chamber: crustal addition, in other words, which need not be directly *"on"* the surface trace of the San Andreas fault.

Let us consider the motion that rapid vertical diapirism 6.5 km west and 18 km below the surface of the San Andreas fault trace should produce. If such diapirism were directed vertically upward from the center of the Earth, it would be inclined 53° from the axis of Earth rotation. The rising diapir would encounter inertial resistance as it rose into higher velocity crust. **Angular momentum would be preserved if the diapir rose not vertically but inclined north of vertical 53°. On that angle the diapiric move-**

ment would parallel Earth's rotational axis; and the ratio of vertical to horizontal motion, cos 53°/sin 53° = .75, a figure that compares rather well with reported Loma Prieta motion: 1.3/1.7 = .76.

Explosively emplaced magma and volatiles at basal crust level may advance upward as breccias and solidified plugs with remaining volatiles. All these are considered diapirs because of their violent method of entry.

Diapirism in this manner can be the basic driver of the San Andreas fault and explain the observed Loma Prieta motions. Diapirism eliminates need for compressional stress. It has the capability of causing right lateral strike-slip motion and rise of west side against east. Diapirism provides an answer to the problem of what happens to 300+ km of horizontal motion where the San Andreas alignment reaches the Mendocino escarpment under the ocean. The answer to this is that local motion measured at any point along the fault would be diverted and diffused into lateral micro-faulting of different orientations along the strike. Hence, quite different net motions should occur along the San Andreas strike. All net San Andreas motion of the San Francisco area would be expected to have been dispersed long before reaching the intersection with the Mendocino escarpment.

Recorded motion on the great fault involves only one sector at a time. This is because only one sector can be close enough to a diapiric intrusion for fault motion to be effected. The closeness factor, and, hence, the length of a sector, will vary according to variable local rock competence.

Diapirism, as motivation for the San Andreas, leads to the conclusion that the "overdue" Parkfield sector may disappoint the hopeful by not moving for a long time. *Movement is only to be expected if intrusive action occurs nearby.*

Like the Parkfield sector, the northern reaches of the fault toward the Mendocino escarpment may be experiencing little diapirism, and hence may be quiescent, and with no activity of any sort, strike or otherwise.

Magmatic vs Mechanical Diapirism

In the case of magmatic intrusion in the San Andreas rift vicinity, the ground surface should be expected to creep with sympathetic motion. No earthquake need occur; but equivalent net strike-slip movement as *slow creeping movement* may occur as the magmatic equivalent of diapirically-caused earthquake displacement.

The "Palmdale bulge" of a few years ago, when the ground rose ominously, illustrates this phenomenon. With the rise, the cognoscenti warned of incipient rupture. Then, after a year or so, just as quietly as it rose, the ground subsided. Intrusion of magma at depth and its subsequent spreading laterally can account for the swell and subsidence.

Diapirism East of the San Andreas Surface Trace

The San Andreas should be thought of as a surface fracture system under which crustal addition occurs. Loci of motions take a planar form with an east dip that is called a "Benioff" zone. Carey interprets this plane as "the boundary of the ascending diapir against the stationary oceanic lithosphere", the new crust surging nappe-like out over oceanic crust. I would add that this Benioff zone likely would have receded progressively eastward as new crust was added. Older additions become atrophied; new, more easterly fractures become new Benioff zones where local regimes of lowered pore pressure, porosity, hydrodynamics of groundwater, and mantle gas emanation accommodate them. Underlying activity in the mantle is fundamental to all of this by providing the energy for spreading and the volatiles and magma as well.

Magmatic intrusion or diapirism in underpressured ground east of the San Andreas fault would have the same tendency to take a northward inclination as its western counterpart; but it would impel left lateral motion uncharacteristic of the San Andreas

fault. **Therefore, insofar as strike-slip motion of the San Andreas fault is originated by intrusion, its earthquake epicenters should be to the west of its slippage surface.**

Jurassic Implications

The great structural S-turn in the "circum-Pacific mega-shear" of S. Warren Carey as shown on Plate III implies right lateral relative motion between the Mendocino and Idaho oroclines. The Sierra Nevada Mountains comprise a 600-km terrane between the Garlock fault on the south and the Mendocino orocline on the north. Its Jurassic melanges and mylonites along with those of western Idaho and the Klamath Mountains originated in Carey's mega-shear.

The diapiric movements in late Jurassic time that created the melanges and the metamorphism of the proto-Sierra Nevada terrane of California compare with deep-seated diapiric activity under the San Andreas at present and over the last 30 million years. The 200-my Sierran diapirism cycle progressed to completion. The present rising mountains result from the vents having become plugged with granites and acidic volcanics, which are the copious melt-products after injection and consolidation of deep-seated ultramafic plutons along with silanes from the inner Earth.

The Jurassic and Cretaceous Benioff zones are interpreted then to have lain eastward under the Sierra Nevada until upwelling volatiles and melted crust had arrived and solidified in such quantities as to cap and seal the vents. That forced the continuing flow of volatiles to seek new openings that by-passed the plugs. The San Andreas rupture zone west of the Sierras and the Mammoth-Long Valley volcanic field on the east are the by-passing sites. The shift of intrusive activity from the Sierras to the Coast Ranges and eastern Sierra, thus, coincided with rising of the mountains.

ROCKY MOUNTAIN STRUCTURES

The literature abounds with studies of the flat faults of the Rocky Mountains. Wyoming, Utah, Montana, Idaho, Alberta, and British Columbia all have these spectacular structures.

Hake, Willis and Addison (1942) astonished the geological profession when they first described the folded thrust faults of the Alberta Rocky Mountains. The Lewis overthrust straddling the U.S./Canada border has a clearly exhibited fault plane that can be seen from the highway, older rock (which makes up the bulk of the higher mountains) having slid eastward over younger rock, perhaps as much as 80 km.

Development of a rationale for Cordilleran arching and shedding of slabs from the roof of the swell became imperative when it was recognized that horizontal piston-like compression is unsustainable for any distance in the Earth's Crust. Geologists had been misled earlier because of the apparent competence of quarried rock. That competence does not exist on a scale of mountain-sized blocks because such blocks are pervasively cracked and jointed.

Theories were slow in coming after 1942, not much being added to our understanding until Hubbert and Rubey (1959) showed conclusively that such faults can move on near-flat slopes under conditions of elevated pore fluid pressure. Fluid pressure explains the behavior of detached slab motion on flat faults such as the Lewis overthrust. Still to be explained was the upward motion of the many secondary "imbricate faults" that are commonly observed in the Rocky Mountains. The behavior of imbricates is one of more westerly slabs repeatedly mounting more easterly neighbors.

The same year as Hubbert and Rubey published their analysis, Wm. C. Gussow, addressing the Alberta Society of Petroleum Geologists asked whether the entire Rocky Mountains might not have been built rapidly. Overnight, he suggested! The surprise and delight of the audience in such an outrageous idea was shown by their reaction - lengthy laughter.

I along with not a few others now think Gussow's suggestion had merit, although we laughed at the time. The scenario most

likely, I now think, is that the terrain of the western ranges and Rocky Mountain trench arched rapidly to a height such that great slabs of sedimentary cover and some basement detached themselves and slid eastward. Each succeeding slab piled into the rear end of the previous one. Momentum caused later-arriving blocks to mount the earlier-arrived ones creating the well known shingle-like, imbricate faulting. Footwall blocks in the imbrications below overriding blocks were "drag-folded" sympathetically.

The systematics of this commonplace faulting are still disputed. Underthrusting of the basement beneath the sedimentary cover from the east is favored by plate tectonics advocates because it offers an ephemeral energy source. Definitive evidence for underthrusting is wholly lacking, however. Arching, on the other hand, with sufficient amplitude for gravity differential to allow a large rock mass to gain enough momentum to mount another block that was acting as an obstacle in its path, is not recognized directly in field evidence either.

I will present evidence that I regard as indisputable in the next section to demonstrate the dilationary activity of this terrain in early Tertiary time. I ask the reader to bear with me for now. With an apology to any who would like me to attack the very vulnerable plate tectonics theory, I regret that doing so would be just too diversionary from my own presention.

Returning to my subject, then, elevation of thrust source area is necessary to initiate gliding and to allow the buildup of momentum of the gliding blocks sufficient for them to mount blocks ahead of them. What means could have provided elevation other than intrusion or dilationary uplift? There being no *surface* indication in the Rocky Mountain trench vicinity of either cryptovolcanism or magmatic intrusion at the Eocene/Oligocene time of Rocky Mountain orogeny, we are stuck with the only remaining endogenic possibility, *dilation of the whole terrain caused by deep-seated diapirism or magma intrusion.*

The last step in the process of Rocky Mountain structural development after the overthrust emplacement was relaxation of the arching. This process induced tensional "normal" faulting in which keystone blocks of the most highly-arched terrain dropped

differentially. Troughs, or "grabens", as geologists call them, offset the overthrusts in this process.

Today we find Oligocene lake beds in some of these troughs, the Flathead valley of southeastern British Columbia being a good example of such a dropped keystone block at the very crest of the present Rockies. The overthrust plate-like preCambrian terrane has been dropped keystone-like into the future Rocky Mountain apex. An Oligocene lake received abundantly fossiliferous sediments (Kishenehn formation) in the resultant depression.

At the time of Cordilleran arching the crest of the dilatancy was somewhat west of the present Rocky Mountain apex. It was approximately at the position of the Rocky Mountain Trench. The trench is, itself, the largest of the dropped keystone blocks. These normal faults and dropped keystone blocks are more common in the trench and western Rocky Mountain ranges than in the imbricate eastern ranges.

Cordilleran arching and relaxation following it must have been brief to satisfy the dynamics and the age constraints of related deposition. **Thrusting age must be less than the late Eocene depositional age of the Saskatchewan Gravels** because those gravels were broadcast across the mountain area *before the mountains rose.* This subject is a major topic under fluviatile cataforms in the next section of this book.

Rocky Mountain orogeny occurred after the broadcast of the Saskatchewan Gravels; and it occurred before the Oligocene lake sedimentation. A brief episode of terrain dilation and relaxation is clearly implied. In the next section I will suggest a possible link to the cataclysmic "event" of the North American tektites of 34 million years ago.

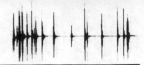

PART II

HYDRAULIC CATAFORMS

ENDOGENY, EXOGENY AND UNIFORMITARIAN
PROCESSES ALL SPAWN
CONSEQUENTIAL PROCESSES, WHICH ARE MANIFEST
AS FLUVIAL SCULPTURE AND DEPOSITION.

In this section we will examine fluvial features that must have entailed so much energy in their origins as to deserve the designation, hydraulic cataforms. Four general categories are recognized. Generic commonality may result in parallel developments of these features, which are:

1. Valley Sculpture
2. Boulder Broadcasts
3. Torrential Flood Deposits
4. Erratics

The layman may be surprised at how much history can be deduced from even a single boulder. Dropped in the mud of the sub-antarctic Weddell Sea a boulder would be an ice-rafted product of water, ice or avalanche, all processes consistent with uniformitarianism.

Put a similar rock without the signs of glacial mauling on a plain or plateau where its arrival cannot be recognized as a gravity induced process and a geological enigma presents itself in confrontation to uniformity, thus creating a challenge to geological ingenuity.

Whether one accepts the challenge is, of course, predicated mainly on whether one is willing to look closely at the facts. Many will not do this, preferring the one-solution-fits-all prescription that uniformitarianism provides. This habit of not questioning dogma is, unfortunately, not confined to the scientific illiterati.

A predilection among geologists to treat myriad surficial deposits of northerly latitudes indiscriminately as products of glaciation is a case in point of the one-solution-fits-all attitude. Tortured terms like "glacio-fluvial" are bandied around, unjustifiably characterizing a petrofabric that is fluvial and glacier-derived. The nearness to a glacier should show up in the terrane analysis, not appended interpretively as a prefix ("glacio") to an otherwise neutral term ("fluvial"). This procedure is wordleading, a prejudicial process of implanting preconception in the reader's mind before the evidence has been presented to him.

All of the phenomena of the coming pages have been dealt with in this sort of prejudiced manner to some degree. And, as a consequence, all have been either prominently misinterpreted or ignored as inconsequential.

VALLEY SCULPTURE

In 1977 I published a paper in the Bulletin of Canadian Petroleum Geology on the age and origin of the interconnected canyon systems of the headwaters of the Columbia and Fraser Rivers of British Columbia, Washington, and Idaho. The study reported on the steep-walled, deep, flat-floored canyons, finding that their infills of Tertiary sediments dated them much earlier than Pleistocene glacial activity, which had cleared out previous canyon fill and exposed the ancient walls. I presented the evidence in the following words:

"Through the Columbia system the deep valleys are floored beneath superficial Quaternary lake, stream, and glacial deposits with Tertiary lake sediments and volcanics. The Tertiary column, which measures in excess of 8,000 ft (2 440 m) in places, seems to be the remains of once-thick valley fills. Regionally the remnants are mainly Oligocene in age. Reports of Oligocene strata have been made for the following areas: on the central Fraser River by Piel (1969, south of Prince George); on the lower Fraser by Fry (1960, above Vancouver); on the Parsnip River in the Rocky Mountain trench by Hopkins (1972, north of Prince George); in the Flathead valley, B.C. by Russell (1964) and P.B. Jones (1969, south of Calgary); and on the Okanagan River, B.C., by A.G.

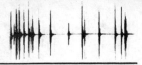

Jones (1959, southeast of Kamloops). Lake beds ranging from late Eocene to probably Miocene are reported on the Okanagan River, B.C. by Duffell and McTaggart (1952) and in various places on Clark Fork, Montana in the Missoula basin by Alden and also by Eakins and Honkala (1952). [Probable] Miocene is reported by Rice (1937) in the Rocky Mountain Trench near Cranbrook, B.C. Pliocene in great thickness is reported in the Bitterroot Valley south of Missoula by Konizeski (1958). Locally the lake beds are interstratified with coarse clastics and volcanics as well as being tilted and eroded."

The analysis shows indisputably that the great Columbia/ Fraser valley system was cut before late Eocene time, a result with profound implications for age interpretations of other valley systems. This revelation discredits entirely the prevailing idea that Pleistocene glaciation was the sole agency for sculpting deep valleys with flat floors, a shibboleth of Quaternary geological theory in our day.

One of the first things the student of physical geology is taught is that hills and valleys are transient, often no older than one million years (Pleistocene), a view supported in numerous cases such as volcanic terranes like Mt. Shasta (400,000 years). He is taught that flat-floored valleys are diagnostic of glacial sculpting. The upper Columbia/Fraser systems show that such is not necessarily the case: the glaciers did scour out *existing valleys* of the Columbia/Fraser system. But valleys were already there ... for fifty million years or more!

Recognition of antiquity in the Columbia and Fraser valley systems came as a revelation to the author, antithetical to his preconception of mountain valleys as essentially young, and glacier-sculpted. This glacier sculpture concept of valleys is widely held without much thought.

In my youth in the California Sierra Nevada, before having studied geology, I remember camp counselors and forest rangers referring to glacial action, always with due respect for the common consensus on the subject. Thusly is popular dogma propagated: innocently, by common consensus, without independent thought, in good faith, even reverently, and not infrequently,

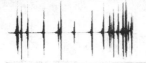

with deadly effect on scientific progress. The solution, Sir Fred Hoyle suggests, is:

> "To adopt the simple precept that whatever is attributed to the current fad is wrong. Experience shows that one is then eventually proved to be correct in nine cases out of ten, a success rate better than anything I have ever been able to achieve by even the most determined burning of midnight oil."

Consider the standard professional view on terrain age in B.C. as expressed by two geologists of the Geological Survey of Canada, J.J. Clague and J.L. Luternauer (1982) in a guidebook to "Late Quaternary Sedimentary Environments, SW British Columbia":

> **"Most landforms and surface sediments in British Columbia are the products of the present interglaciation and the late Wisconsin (Fraser) glacial cycle."**

How totally incorrect that statement is with respect to landforms! These geologists simply have not really considered the landform information ... as I had not before my Inundation paper [which they do not cite ... and likely have not read].

Once having recognized the deficiency in understanding of the Columbia valleys, it was a short step to try the same trick in other mountainous terranes. Surprising results were in store.

Klamath Mountains Sculpture

In the Klamaths the applicability was immediately apparent on cursory inspection: Cretaceous sedimentary inliers establish minimum Cretaceous ages for the valleys in which they are deposited. These valley ages imply similar minimum ages for some other valleys and interfluvial uplands of the same terrane.

This unexpected valley antiquity of the deeply-incised Klamaths can be mistaken, even less than the Columbia/Fraser valleys, for ice sculpture. There was little Quaternary glaciation

and none in the Tertiary or Cretaceous in this terrane, at least not affecting middle and lower elevations.

Sierra Nevada Sculpture

Sheer rock walls of the Columbia/Fraser system give evidence of Pleistocene ice scouring, but were not created in that way. Similar sheer rock walls in the Sierra Nevada Mountains, [Yosemite valley or Kings Canyon, for example] dissect and drain topographically mature uplands not unlike those of the Columbia/Fraser system. The uplands were said by my teacher on that subject (J.P. Buwalda) to be Miocene in age.

The Yuba River system of the northern Sierra, a terrane of placer gold fame, is an incised Eocene-age river system that was flooded with lavas in Miocene time and forced to relocate its water courses. The channels of the auriferous gravels of the northern Sierra are interpreted to be Eocene in age, which then is the likely minimum age of the interfluvial uplands. Throughout the Sierra Nevada these are likely all of the same age, remnants of a mature Eocene or perhaps Cretaceous land surface.

Canyon-cutting Mechanisms

Canyon sculpture is carried out by just two general mechanisms, (1) glacial ice with entrained rock and (2) flowing water with entrained rock. As previously mentioned, ice (at mid-to-lower altitudes) is not a feasible agency for deep canyon cutting in Tertiary or Cretaceous times in any of the terranes being discussed. Water with entrained rock is necessarily the agency of choice in all cases.

Columbia/Fraser Situation

Scenic grandeur of the upper Columbia/Fraser valley system forces upon us the question, "Why would water cut very deep

SCENE 8

THREE VALLEY GAP, BRITISH COLUMBIA

Flat-floored, steep-walled valley incised into mature upland. Perched valley fill on right has been bypassed by late glacial scouring.

canyons?" A "normal" dendritic watershed would have narrow fast-flowing streams and V-shaped canyons. Interfluvial erosion would keep up, furnishing all the detritus the streams could transport. Valleys would not widen until maturity was reached. Never would "normal" runoff result in streams able to erode deep flat-floored canyons.

Between deep canyons the interfluvial upland of the Columbia/Fraser drainage retains its deeply weathered and chemically altered surface, an "etchplain" in Budel's terminology. This is a deeply weathered stable surface subject mainly to ongoing chemical attack. Ordinarily an etchplain is only very slowly modified by chemical action excepting at its edges, where it slumps into encroaching drainage systems.

If the flat-floored Eocene or Cretaceous valleys with precipitous scenery along the Trans Canada Highway between Sicamous and Revelstoke could not have developed from erosion by meteoric waters or ice what then would have cut them out? The hydraulic

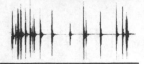

SCENE 8

Closeup views of the unstratified gravel deposit shown above. Lacking stratification this deposit could be interpreted as a glacial till or torrential flood deposit. The boulders and cobbles are entirely quartzite and all well-rounded, identical to the Saskatchewan Gravels of the prairies.

Glacial origin is precluded because of (1) absence of the mixed rock types of the terrain over which the glacier of this site flowed and (2) absence of glacial striae or chattermarks on the clasts. This gravel must be a remnant of the boulder broadcast and valley scouring "event" of Eocene times.

dilemma is that valleys cannot be widened to the stage of exhibiting flat floors unless mass wasting and avalanching of valley walls can be constrained while valley widening takes place or lateral erosion at the bottom is effectively speeded up. This latter would be possible if conditions of surging and turbulent flow with entrained rock were introduced so as to provide rapid corrasive action.

I proposed extraordinary tidal action with a bed load of quartzite boulders to scour out the channels. That still looks to me

SCENE 8

Closeup of gravel, at base of erosional scarp.

as the only available solution. It is both necessary and sufficient to solve the problem.

Curiously, the boulder valley fill one km west of Three Valley Gap on the Trans Canada Highway is made up of the required quartzite boulders. Perhaps it is a remnant of the original cutting agent. (Photo scene 8).

Yosemite, a Contrasting Situation

By contrast, an excavated valley providing similar superficial evidence can be examined readily in Yosemite Valley, California.

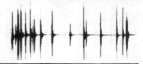

Scene 9

"LAKE YOSEMITE"

A painting depicting the Pleistocene lake as imagined by Francois E. Matthes. Note the mature upland surface.

That valley has moraines and glacial lake sediments dated to the last 85,000 years. But the excavated valley (700 m deep) is three-quarters filled with earlier sediments that represent about one million years at present rates of valley filling.

Pervasive glaciation of uplands and valleys in the Yosemite area renders the evidence ambiguous as to valley origin. It seems safe to say that a developed Tertiary river system must have been in place before ice age accentuation of scenery took place. It is unlikely that southern Sierran Eocene or Cretaceous drainage would have been replaced as in the Yuba system, because basalt flows did not block the drainage, as they did in the north.

Thus, at Yosemite, unlike the B.C. example, glacial processes appear to have been the main sculpting agency of the U-shaped valley, although definitive evidence has not been found. The idea, which the B.C. example discredits, that a U-shaped valley necessarily defines a glacial origin, is faulty: a flat-floored valley may be either fluvial or glacial in origin.

The Baraboo Situation

Crickmay in his book, "The Work of the River", provides a compelling example of the preservation of ancient topography, this one five hundred million years in age:

> "..in the Baraboo Ranges of Wisconsin, shallow flat-bottomed valleys are incised into low uplands of Precambrian quartzite; their floors are carpeted (so to speak) wall to wall with a thin deposit of Cambrian sandstone. Evidently enough, the valleys were there at the beginning of the Paleozoic [and] have not [changed] in five hundred million years." [p184]

Crickmay's concept is that great differences prevail in the rates of landscape reduction, 1 to 1,000,000 being not unusual. A rapid degradation by meteoric waters and ice in mountainous terrain would be perhaps one million times faster than the rate of erosion of gentle prairieland [such as Alberta prairies], where the land surface is substantially protected by vegetation from ablation.

Crickmay uses the term "stagnant" for the non-eroding terrain, which seems immune to measurable erosion. Interestingly, Budel in his book, Climatic Geomorphology, ascribes another form of long-term stability to the steep slopes of "inselbergs" ("island mountains"). These features rise as near-vertical walls from flat desert surfaces. Budel shows that insignificant erosion of these slopes occurs over great periods of time.

Both Budel and Crickmay impute fuzzy thinking as the culprit for widespread misperception of the terrain age and its evolutionary process. The references in this book to "young-looking" mountain valleys that are in reality very old, also arise from that cause. Not only Budel's inselberg slopes but our valleys illustrate with elegance the Crickmay "theory of unequal activity."

Crickmay attributes the mistaken notion that all terrain is being inexorably eroded and by imputation at similar rates, to the Lyellian idea that there is "no repose on the face of the Earth, all surficial process [being] continuous." Crickmay's theory contributes for our solution the proposition that *rates of erosion of slope and valley bottom may be grossly unequal.*

Whereas Crickmay's gentle Cambrian valleys were created by "normal" Lyellian uniformitarian riverine erosion, suspension of activity for one-half billion years denies the generality of Lyell's theory. The age of the valleys of B.C. similarly flies in the face of unending change. Not only are we faced with stalled erosional processes on the valley walls, but on the interfluvial uplands as well. Near stasis has prevailed since Eocene times.

So much for the age of the hills and valleys. How old are they? Often very old. Much older than we thought.

Excavation of the deep valleys required a sufficiently high rate of down-cutting that mass-wasting and avalanching of walls could not keep up with it. How was rapid widening of valley floors and slope-base erosion accomplished? **Excluding glaciers, only slurries of coarse gravel held in suspension by turbulence could have achieved this end.**

In my 1977 paper I proposed that enormous tides must have prevailed, swirling in and out for a sufficient time to effect valley cutting. It is difficult to imagine any adequate substitute among known processes. **The tide mechanism is really the only choice.**

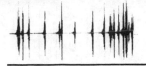

BOULDER BROADCASTS

These features have further tales to tell. It is intriguing that quartz and quartzite boulders predominate in some old accumulations where they are foreign to or deficient in the host terrane.

Sierran Yuba Valley Fill

The ancestral Yuba River system of the northern Sierra Nevada, California is one of these. The so-called "auriferous gravel" from which the '49ers extracted nugget gold is nearly 100% water-worn rounded quartz gravel. The gravel deposits are cradled in aggraded shallow valleys cut into Sierran granites and motherlode series metasedimentary rocks. Basalt caps above the auriferous gravels were created by lava flowing down the stream courses. Where the quartz came from and why there is no granite contribution in the auriferous deposits are engaging problems. The quartz is thought to be derived from pre-volcanic vein quartz secreted from vents that were later obliterated by volcanic action.

Columbia/Fraser: Valley Fill

The headwaters region of the Columbia/Fraser system in its upper reaches has boulder accumulations, which are not traceable to precise sources. The lithology is ortho-quartzite (former sedimentary rock); and the boulder form is often cannonball roundness. These boulders predominate among the very coarse fraction of valley fills in the deep valleys along the Sicamous-Revelstoke stretch of the Trans Canada Highway.

High-grade metamorphics and intrusives of the "Shuswap terrane" are the lithologies of the bedrock adjacent to the highway and beneath the valley fills. These are gneisses (high-grade granitized metamorphic rocks) deficient in clean quartzites.

Continental Divide: Quartzite Gravels

Beside the Trans Canada Highway on Kicking Horse Pass some 150 km from the Sicamous-Revelstoke area, rounded quartzite cobbles occur in ill-sorted unconsolidated surficial deposits. This is the "main ranges" terrane of the Rockies, where quartzite boulders and cobbles also occur lithified into thick lower Cambrian conglomerates (Gog and related formations). Whether the surficial Pass deposits are reworked Gog or eastwardly transported correlatives of the Three Valley Gap quartzite gravels is unclear at this time.

Oregon: Quartzite Gravels

Far to the south in the Wallowa Mountains of central Oregon Allen reports that:

"Beneath the [Miocene age] basalt cap of Lookout Mountain [resting on granite] at 8,800-feet elevation, a 50-foot-thick bed of river gravel contains giant quartzite boulders that can only have come from far to the east in the Rockies."

The extensive volcanism of the Columbia/Fraser systems downstream from their headwaters regions renders obscure the full extent of quartzite gravel broadcasts. But it is apparent that they must have been very extensive.

Canadian Prairies: Quartzite Gravels

Fortunately, a better preservation record occurs east of the continental divide on the Canadian prairies, where the same lithology, clasts in places up to one metre in diameter, and the same high degree of rounding shows up to dominate the terraces and banks of eastwardly-flowing Alberta rivers, the Bow and Saskatchewan systems.

The gravel has formation status, being known as the Saskatchewan Gravels. It occurs in central and southern Alberta and southern Saskatchewan beneath the glacial deposits and above Paleocene bedrock of the Paskapoo formation.

There is no possible local quartzite source for this rock, and geologists have long regarded it as a river-transported product from the west that arrived before the mountains rose during the Eocene "Laramide orogeny."

In southern Alberta the gravel size diminishes eastward. It has been partly redistributed in the Eocene Swift Current formation, which makes up river terraces of Oligocene, Miocene, and Pliocene ages. Later reworking occurs in Pleistocene tills and torrential flood deposits. Remnants of the earliest broadcast deposits are only preserved perched on higher ground.

The boulder broadcast occurred over erosional topography of at least hundreds of metres of relief, and patches of that radiation occur in notches and depressions of the paleo-terrain. In the Calgary area such occurrences have been exposed on Nosehill. Other major remnants of the broadcast occur on plateaus as outliers. The Cypress Hills in far southeast Alberta and the Hand Hills of central Alberta are capped with such outliers. In the Cypress Hills the blanket reaches a thickness of 15 m in places with boulders up to .3 m in diameter.

Tills of the prairies incorporate varying quantities of the gravels admixed with Canadian shield rock supplied by the continental glaciers and with Rocky Mountain rock of glacial or fluvial origin from the west. In the Calgary area the bed load gravels of the Glenmore torrential flood deposit, which is to be discussed in detail in the third division of Part II, page 108, is gravel mainly of this provenance.

Saskatchewan Gravels, Cypress Hills

The most easterly prominent remnant of the original boulder broadcast, the erosional outlier capping the Cypress Hills of southeast Alberta, is 300 km from the continental divide and, presently 1 500 m above sea level. This deposition is today 850 m

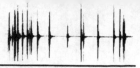
above the upper Columbia/Fraser valley bottom elevations, where the gravels are presumed to have originated.

The large expanse of nearly pure quartz boulders is up to fifteen metres in thickness. Perhaps originally laid in a depression, the deposit has protected the underlying clays from erosion.

The huge energy requirement for transporting the coarse boulder load from its source west of the continental divide implies a single hyper-energy event. The earliest timing for this event is constrained in southern Alberta by the Paleocene Paskapoo formation, on which the gravels were deposited. The latest timing is constrained by the redepositional age of the fraction that shows up in the Eocene Swift Current formation. These constraints establish a late Paleocene or early Eocene age for the boulder broadcast.

The possibility is open that the prairie boulder broadcast was contemporary with valley development in the Columbia/Fraser River systems.

The lithology requires a western source, and delivery required extraordinary energy in order to have suspended large rounded boulders for the time and distance of delivery.

Broadcast of a blanket of boulders over the 375-km distance from the Rocky Mountain trench across a surface with little if any negative slope, must have required hyper-energy flooding. The blanket then is a cataform.

Caribou Plateau Gravels

The Caribou Mountains, in far northern Alberta, comprise a 3 800 km² plateau situated north of, and 500 metres above, the Peace River, which flows eastward some 25 km south of the plateau's edge. The entire area of the large plateau is carpeted with highly rounded boulders of red Canadian Shield granite and other metamorphic rock, all of which is quite foreign to the late Cretaceous shale terrane. Clasts up to one metre in diameter are not uncommon.

Erosional encroachment on the edges of the plateau allows the profusion of boulders to slump into the encroaching creeks,

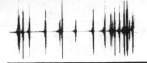

choking their flow. Eventually reaching the Peace, Slave, or Hay Rivers, the boulders trail off downstream, lining the riverbanks far down the Mackenzie to the Arctic Ocean.

The 500-metre-thick blanket of Cretaceous shale removed by erosion from around the Caribou Mountains plateau in Cenozoic time was accomplished by runoff and soil slumpage at the edges of the plateau *since* the boulder emplacement. Glacial effects have been minor by comparison.

The Caribou boulders are unlike the highly rounded quartzite clasts of the Saskatchewan Gravels. They have a dark brown surface patina, a thin coating much resembling desert varnish, over fresh rock, which is usually within a millimetre of the surface. The clast surfaces are pitted by an earlier stage of differential weathering. The pits are painted over with the brown patina, which has a silk-smooth texture. There are no glacial striae or chattermarks from the grinding action of ice-encased rock against bedrock or other ice-encased clasts. Well-rounded edges characterize the boulders, but seldom reach the cannonball roundness found in the Saskatchewan Gravels.

In summary, then, the Caribou Mountains boulders are apparently not ice-transported, they are provenance of the Canadian shield, and they must have been emplaced since the deposition of the bedrock shales in Cretaceous time and before Oligocene time, when the surrounding broad valley erosion commenced.

The height of the plateau is 500 m or so above the nearest Canadian Shield granite source area to the east. Thus the plateau was likely lower when the boulders were delivered. But there is no evidence suggesting sufficient elevation differential for the boulders to have moved by everyday river processes from a shield source. Delivery of the Caribou boulders would have required turbulence and a westward-moving flood.

Recognized prominent extraordinary pre-Pleistocene violent events that could have affected this location in the fifty million years of post-Paleocene Cenozoic time are three in number. They are the Columbia/Fraser valley cutting, the Saskatchewan Gravels boulder broadcast, and the impact that produced the North American tektite strewnfield. All are Eocene in age; only the tektite member is a primary "event."

The valley-cutting mechanism might offer some possibility for association if a tidal mechanism across essentially flat ground could be imagined. That does not seem possible as the shield, while having low relief, was not flat, and the Caribou plateau area was not likely a depression that could receive boulders from tidal surging.

The Saskatchewan Gravels boulder broadcast was *from the west* and must have been a consequence of a different "event."

North American Tektites and the Caribou Boulders

Harold C. Urey (1973) originated the idea of an impact causing the North American tektite array. He said it resulted in widespread extinctions, especially to 70% of radiolarians. The mass of North American tektites, one billion tonnes according to Glass (1986), represents about 0.4 km³ of rock splashed half way or more around the world. Micro-tektites and glass spherules found in deepsea cores augment the splashed volume to eight billion tonnes, which originated according to Ganapathy (1982) with a chondritic (stony) impactor of 3-km diameter, 14 km³ in rock volume.

The impact splashed molten rock beyond the atmosphere. The tektite fallback comprised two fractions that have been identified, one that landed after congealing in atmospheric flight, the other that congealed in atmospheric flight, left the atmosphere, and remelted and recongealed on reentry before landing. Much material must have passed beyond the gravitational field. Ocean floor coring, on which Ganapathy relied, has revealed microtektites, glass spherules, and siderophile metals in the fallback deposit. These are attributed to the extraterrestrial contribution from the impactor.

The tsunamis that would have ensued from this impact would have been enormous. Radiating from the impact site, they would have encircled the globe and swept over entire continents gaining ferocity like breakers on the beach as their energy was concentrated by shallowing conditions.

The boulder broadcast of the Saskatchewan Gravels was the sort of cataform to be expected from an *eastward-traveling wave front* that had passed over mostly-submerged British Columbia, swept up a gravel mass collected on the shoal of the rising Rocky Mountains, and spread it eastward across the Alberta prairies. That wave must then have preceded the building of the Rocky Mountains.

The Caribou plateau "event" required a *westward-traveling wave front.* I suggest the most prospective location for this impact is Greenland. The island has a central depression that reaches 100 m below sea level. It is elongate, trending north-south and rimmed by mountains 1 000-2 000 m in height on all sides.

The Greenland crater form could have been produced by a very large Apollo asteroid traveling southward nearly tangential to Earth's surface. The grazing impact in a shallow ocean floored with a thin sedimentary veneer over submerged crystalline shield could have splashed melted crust at escape velocities and produced the North American tektite shower and the Caribou tsunami wave front. The wave evidently swept across Labrador, Baffin Island, Hudsons Bay, and the Canadian barrenlands, picking up stream boulders from those stagnant terrains and broadcasting them across low-lying northern Alberta.

Three Valley Gap Gravels

What comparison can be made between lithology and rock types where we first discussed boulders, along the Trans Canada Highway, and the prairie occurrences? The best location is one km west of Three Valley Gap. There, off-white quartzites identical in appearance to the Cypress Hills boulders comprise a perched valley fill beside the highway. The site is a particularly good exposure, 100 m thick, unsorted, with clasts up to one metre in size. Late Wisconsin erosion by water or glacier ice has cut off the valley, exposing the fill (Photo scene 8).

Common Origins of Gravels

Popular belief interprets this quartzite to originate from pre-Cambrian metasedimentary formations (Belt supergroup, Shuswap terrane etc.). Riverine corrasive rounding is presumed to explain the production process, although this attribution appears flawed due to sheer gravel volume. My carbide-hydride systematics offer a better alternative (Part III).

Extreme rounding of a very large quantity of rock is much more apt to occur in a seashore environmemt than in rivers. The difference in addition to the volume is that rivers produce mixtures of local and far-travelled clasts, some angular, some rounded. The sheer volume of boulders comprising the broadcast blanket is far greater than the several ancestral eastward-flowing rivers could have produced on low gradients. Riverine processes, therefore, are less apt to produce either the perfection and uniformity of rounding or the quantity of these boulders, whereas seashores habitually do just that.

Let us consider the quantities of rock. Many rivers of central and southern Alberta are choked with it; all have some of it. Linings of riverbeds and concentrations in terraces and bars as much as 20 m in thickness are not unusual.

The Three Valley Gap occurrence is typical of the gravel in easterly British Columbian valleys. The typical clasts trail down the Columbia into Montana, Idaho, and Washington and down the Fraser system of British Columbia, where they soon become diluted with locally derived debris.

The amount of preserved gravel in the Pacific watershed in Canada is less by far than that to the east of the continental divide. The prairie deposits, eastwardly distributed far from any possible source, owe their preservation to the low level of erosional activity in the Cenozoic prairie environment.

If we suppose that the mass of gravel now found east of the Rockies came from a single beach system located on an 800-km shoal along the axis of the Rocky Mountains in Canada and Montana, and that this gravel shoal was transported in Eocene time by a great eastward-moving wave that broadcast the boulders

in a blanket averaging one metre thickness over an area of 800 x 400 km² on the prairies, then later Cenozoic erosion could have effected redistributions and reworking of the boulders to achieve the present uneven distribution.

The volume of the gravel blanket would have been 200 km³, 0.25 km³ per linear km of shoal. If shoal width had been, let us say, 20 km, average gravel depth would have been 12.5 metres on the 800-km length in Cretaceous time, a massive gravel bar by any measure. The 20-km bar width could have been generated by a westwardly regressive strandline. Successive lower-level bar elements would have been developed and abandoned as the seashore receded westward.

Transfer in a slurry of the enormous 200-km³ gravel bar from its origins on the rising swell of the Canadian Rockies to its new prairie abode would have necessitated turbulence sufficient to carry the coarsest 35-cm boulders 300-500 km across nearly flat ground. This implies sudden and massive energy input. A huge wave front inundating the entire western part of Canada and the adjoining United States is suggested. Nothing less would seem adequate to carry the coarse boulder load so far.

The argument will be advanced by those anxious to avoid the hyper-energy wave interpretation that rivers could have performed the original transport and later streams or glaciers dispersed the rock. These assertions are superficially attractive until one takes into account that there is not adequate slope for 300-500 km of eastward riverine translocation of 35-cm boulders. Existing rivers on their present gradients would not be sufficiently energetic. More elevation of the source area would be required.

In the present river systems the larger boulders hardly move seaward at all due to insufficient fluvial energy. Post-Eocene river gradients are moderately well understood from the clast sizes of their deposits, none of which has the coarse texture of the Saskatchewan or Caribou gravels. Thus, post-Eocene streams have been no more energetic than present rivers.

The option of river transport for the Saskatchewan and Caribou gravels would demand two separate episodes of Eocene uplift, one for the Rockies and one for the Shield. *Such uplift lasting for any significant time span would have resulted in deltas being*

built downstream from the course gravel deposition. We should find remnants of an eastward-directed delta on the preCambrian Shield and in Hudson Bay carrying fines of the Saskatchewan Gravels and of a westward-directed delta in northern Alberta bearing shield-derived debris. That these are not found negates the uplift theory.

Short-lived dilation events for these gravels deserve attention, however, because of the interpretation (See Part I) of similar dilation in the terminal Eocene "event." A great Eocene dilation created the Cordillera, the spine of North America, where nothing comparable had existed before. The dilation/relaxation process must have been short-lived.

Thus I would argue, that **hyper-energy is necessary to explain both the canyon-excavating by tidal surging and the boulder broadcast on the Canadian prairies. The former would have required extreme tidal surging over millenia. The latter could have resulted either from a single tsunami or from brief uplift that was soon relaxed.** The tsunami alone could have broadcast the boulders; dilation would have required additional fluvial energy to assimilate and broadcast them.

The best fit among facts is that the **quartzite gravels of the upper Columbia/Fraser valley system comprised the cutting agent with which tidal oscillations over millenia carved out the Columbia/Fraser valley system of British Columbia, Idaho, Washington, and western Montana. At an unknown stage in the surging, a massive wave front swept boulder accumulations eastward from the crest of the rising Rockies. Later, a westward-moving wave swept across the shield, broadcasting shield boulders westward across the northern part of the Alberta basin.**

Summarized Gravel Ages

Surging and canyon cutting in the Columbia and Fraser rivers' headwaters terrain could have started at K/T time or in the late Paleocene or early Eocene. Saskatchewan Gravels must be late Paleocene or Eocene. The Caribou plateau gravels are of uncertain but probable Eocene age, possibly correlating with the 34-million-year-old North American tektite strewnfield.

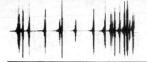

The origin of the Saskatchewan Gravel quartzites, as earlier mentioned, is usually attributed to the late preCambrian Belt supergroup. No specific source has been identified, and the attribution is unconvincing upon comparison with Belt exposures. The latter prominently include bright hues (green, lavender, red, brown) as well as the drab or off-white character of the Saskatchewan Gravels.

Their best lithologic correlation is the conglomerate clasts of the lower Cambrian Gog formation of the Rocky Mountain main ranges. Both the subdued colors and high degree of rounding are a match. The source of Gog quartzite clasts is, however, no clearer than for the Saskatchewan Gravels. Beltian or earlier age is required for the derivation, and Gog-age (preCambrian-Cambrian transition to lower Cambrian) is the indicated time of the first stage of rounding. This was advanced to some degree on the Cretaceous shoal in a later stage of rounding.

Thus, in summary, Saskatchewan and Three Valley Gap gravels may have been generated from preCambrian sources at pC/C time, then protected by incorporation in the Cambrian Gog terrane until exposed and re-concentrated into a great beach or bar on the Eocene arch of the future Rocky Mountains. Their availability for assimilation into an advancing tsunami or for being swept by meteoric runoff was set up before the late Eocene events that included their redeposition.

Sierran Yuba Gravel Age

It is interesting that the auriferous quartz gravels of the Sierra Nevada, which in their rounding resemble the prairie quartzite gravels, have been correlated with quartz arenites of the upper Eocene Ione formation of California's Great Valley sequence. The Ione is an Eocene marine formation with a tropical microfauna. These curious coincidences in time and lithology between Sierran auriferous gravel and Saskatchewan Gravel are reported without any suggestion of a link. My carbide-hydride theory (Part III) suggests that one may, in fact, exist, however.

TORRENTIAL FLOOD DEPOSITS

The Glenmore Stratum of the Calgary Silt

Youthful torrential flood deposits are to be found that avoid the inherent lack of datable content. One of these is the Glenmore stratum of the Calgary Silt formation within the City of Calgary, Alberta. My interest in the Calgary Silt stemmed from the perception that the Foothills Erratics Train (taken up ahead) is deposited on or within it.

Having published a paper on the subject in 1977 and asserted the likelihood of the two being contemporaneous, on hearing a report in 1981 that mammalian fossils had been found in the silt, I followed it up. The report turned out to be false (the fossils were imposed and younger), but in the course of checking the lead, charcoal was found in the silt and dated. The result was an age of 26,000 years before present ("yBP").

As the Erratics Train is interpreted generally as the last event of Wisconsin glaciation, 11,000 yBP more or less, the new Silt age is 15,000 years earlier. Let us now examine this phenomenon in more detail.

The Calgary Silt is an ubiquitous mantle under the mainly residential districts of the city. Its lateral extent outside Calgary is unknown. The silt is water-laid and varies to more than 50 m in thickness over the underlying topography.

The site of investigation was the lake bank immediately west of the parking lot of the Rockyview Hospital, a convenient location for study purposes south of Bow River. The bevelled upper surface of Paleocene Paskapoo bedrock topography is found in contact with the overlying silt mantle. Lake waters have exposed the contact in several places.

At one point a large (1 m) boulder of Paskapoo sandstone, striated by glacial scour on its former upper surface, has been overturned and submerged in Calgary Silt. Above the Paskapoo, 30 metres of unstratified and slightly consolidated bouldery silt is exposed in banks that are actively caving as the recently dammed lake undermines them. The silt is featureless, sandy, calcareous, and barren of megafossils. The only microfauna found in the silt is

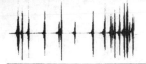

Trochammina sp., a Cretaceous form with agglutinated siliceous wall structure (courtesy of J.H. Wall, Geol. Surv. Can.).

The most interesting aspects of the Calgary Silt are its boulder and charcoal contents. Boulders are abundant in the lowest metre or so, but sparser upward until only odd cobbles and pebbles occur in the silt three or four metres above the base (photo scene 10).

The boulders are from the Saskatchewan Gravels boulder broadcast. Almost all are highly-rounded quartzite identical to the boulder fraction in the nearby river terraces and to perched deposits as found on the Cypress Hills. Most of the rounded-quartzite boulders have polished and pitted surfaces, the pits apparently caused by impacts that marred the otherwise almost mirror surfaces.

A minor complement of boulder clasts comprises decaying granite or schist, likely a glacial or peri-glacial (ice-rafted) contribution from the Canadian Shield. A third fraction, also minor, is Rocky Mountain sedimentary rock.

The boulders and pebbles are matrix-supported, indicating significant deposition of silt before the boulders settled out. Matrix support in a "massive" deposit, which is wholly devoid of any vestige of bedding, indicates a very turgid slurry such that silt at lower levels had settled enough that boulders raining down from above could not settle through it. This is a major clue to the nature of the Calgary flood of 26,000 yBP.

As previously mentioned, the silt has a sparse Cretaceous microfauna. It would seem reasonable that such fossils could have been picked up as the flood progressed over bevelled Cretaceous shaly country rock. Scattered in the silt are flecks and lumps of charcoal. The possible origins of this material should be another clue to the nature of the flood.

As mentioned, I had the charcoal dated by the carbon-14 method. Geochron Laboratories of Cambridge, Massachusetts provided the specific result of 25,850 + 1,780 to − 1,460 B.P.

Boulder sizes allow a crude estimation of slurry velocity. For .3 to .5 metre boulders, the largest observed in this outcrop, the velocity of the flood must have been 10-15 km/h to carry the boulders in suspension. From this data we can gain some insight into the water volume involved in the torrential flood that emplaced the Calgary Silt.

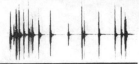

SCENE 10

CALGARY "SILT"

Above: Water-rounded cobbles and boulders suspended in silt.
Below: Basal unconformity with Paleocene Paskapoo sandstone.

SCENE 10

BOULDERS OF PRECAMBRIAN QUARTZITE

These boulders have successively been incorporated into at least five different sedimentary formations. The larger boulders are about 65 cm in diameter. Their rounding was originally the work of lower Cambrian shoreline processes but may have been enhanced in the development of late Cretaceous beaches as the sea receded from the rising arch of the Rocky Mountains.

Originating in the preCambrian/Cambrian transition, the boulders were first incorporated into a conglomerate of lower Cambrian age, the Gog formation of the main ranges of the Canadian Rockies. In Cretaceous time the Gog was reduced by erosion, its boulders being reconcentrated as beach deposits. The beaches were abandoned by the receding Cretaceous sea and left as a great mound of gravel on the axis of the present Rocky Mountains.

In Eocene times this bar was swept eastward across the Alberta prairies by a hyper-energy wave and left as the boulder broadcast known as the Saskatchewan Gravels. Middle and later Tertiary erosion lowered these members of the boulder broadcast by letdown into river bank deposits of the Bow River as the river valley was cut into the prairie terrain. In late Pleistocene time, 26,000 years ago, they were again swept up in a turbulent flood and deposited with silt and charcoal of the flood as the "Glenmore stratum" of the Calgary Silt.

Here on the shore of the Glenmore reservoir, the boulders have been winnowed out of the easily-eroded Calgary Silt by the waters of the reservoir lapping against its banks.

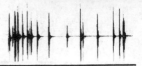

First, however, let us look into the channel this torrent must have occupied. Glacier distribution at this time was the controlling factor. Mountain glaciers flowed eastward out of Rocky Mountain valleys. The continental ice sheet encroached on the Calgary area from the northeast, its center being near Hudson Bay.

River runoff from the Rockies was unable to flow as it does today to Hudson Bay. In central and southern Alberta water flow was diverted south into the Mississippi system. Farther north it was diverted into the Mackenzie River, likely via the Liard tributary of the Mackenzie. The Peace and Athabaska rivers that now handle most northern Alberta runoff are thought to have been blocked by Wisconsin ice in the same manner as the more southerly Saskatchewan, Red Deer and Bow river systems.

The ice-free corridor (Fig. 3) that ran south-southeastward along the Rocky Mountain front, approximately perpendicular to the courses of all the rivers flowing out of the Rocky Mountains, served to conduct the diverted river waters of the Athabaska, Saskatchewan, Red Deer and Bow rivers past Calgary. In all likelihood the corridor was open from the Arctic to Montana (White et al, 1979), although the connection from the Peace River north to the Liard, a tributary to the Mackenzie, is not yet proved.

The west side of the ice-free corridor comprised foothills of the Rockies or the montane glaciers that flowed from them. The glaciers from the west encroached on the ice-free corridor, which was the scene of much ponding and erratic runoff in a southeasterly direction. New channels were often cut outside the pre-existing deeply-incised drainage system. Since topographic relief of the river valleys is 50-150 m, the diversion of the river flow would result in lakes of those depths. Some sites of deposition of the Calgary Silt show the thin repetitive layers known as varves that are indicative of lake deposition. The Glenmore site does not exhibit varves.

The channels that were eroded into the floor of the ice-free corridor are now abandoned but are still readily visible as "dry valleys" (Photo scene 11). The ice-free corridor must have been used whenever continental ice blocked the main river systems of

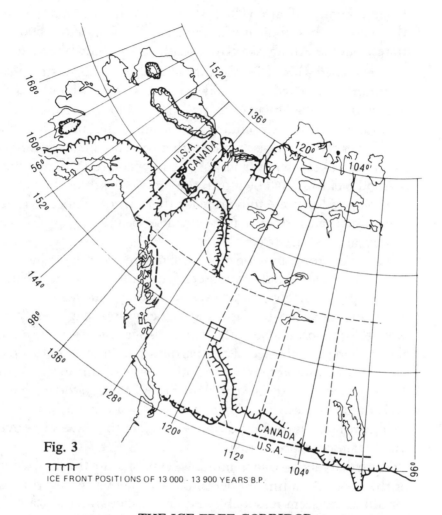

Fig. 3

ICE FRONT POSITIONS OF 13 000 - 13 900 YEARS B.P.

THE ICE-FREE CORRIDOR

From White et al (1979). Square shows White study area in which there occurs continuous lake sedimentation dated through the last 30,000 years. The probability seems high that contiguity existed between the ice-free corridors reaching north from southern Alberta and south from the arctic plains.

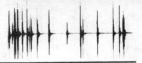

the prairies. It provided the course of movement of the later Alberta Erratics Train (Plate I), the distinctive remnants of which are the best indicator of the exact location of the 600-km route from the Athabaska River south to the Montana border.

The incised Bow River valley at Calgary and upstream at Cochrane is flanked by boulder terraces from which I have collected Pliocene ungulate bones. The said terraces are themselves much below surrounding prairieland. The incising by the Bow River of its valley is at least earlier than the Pliocene terrace fauna, and likely much older, as the Pliocene terraces are more than 80% of the way down into the incised depth of the valley. The deep valleys were fully in place then, before Pliocene time, five million years, that is, and, of course, before the 26,000-year torrential flood occurred.

The flood front, moving along the ice-free corridor transverse to the Bow valley, would have ascended the 50-metre south bank, behaving predictably like a wave mounting and overtopping a beach or strandline bar, gaining velocity and amplitude as it mounted the beach obstacle, then dissipating its energy and clastic burden in the lee of the barrier. The implied *direction of wave propagation had to be southward* because of this mechanism. The silt might have been stirred up from Cretaceous bedrock and Pleistocene tillites. The boulder burden may have been only assimilated locally, a short distance ahead of the wave surge over the Glenmore deposition site.

With that mechanism in mind, we can estimate the dimensions of the flood. A minimum depth of 50 m above the obstructing terrain would seem reasonable. An average channel width of 20 km fits known facts, and a minimum flow rate of 15 km/h average would give 4 167 000 m ^{3}/s (141,000,000 cfs or 3,237 acre-ft/s) as flow volume.

Jarratt & Malde (1987) report on comparative flood events as follows: The greatest flood of recorded history, the Amazon flood, 1953, discharged 385 000 m³/s, or about 10% of the Calgary figure. The Lake Bonneville discharge (more on this later) at 935 000 m³/s would be 40 % of the Calgary figure. But Lake Missoula's discharge (also, more later) would have exceeded all others with a probable 15 000 000 m³/s, 350% of the Calgary figure.

SCENE 11

A "DRY VALLEY"

Eroded into prairieland as a southward diversion channel for the combined runoff of the eastern slopes of the Alberta Rocky Mountains, the channel has been abandoned and without a river for the last 11,000 years.

Although the size of boulders in this deposit shows that slurry density had to be sufficient for silt to deposit beneath boulders in the settling process, slurry density did not approach that of a lahar where boulders end up dispersed throughout the fabric of the deposit. The density then must have been just sufficient to provide matrix support for the boulders in the lowest few metres of deposition.

What terrain gradients could have been involved in this flood other than the local gradients of the Bow Valley? In the grand perspective the Calgary site is about equidistant (4 000 km or so) from tidewater on the Arctic Ocean and Gulf of Mexico. It is 1 000 m higher.

The two largest comparative floods mentioned by Jarratt and Malde maintained energy by having steep negative gradients and much shorter flow courses than 4 000 km. The routes those floods took are well posted with the evidence of their passage. The ice-free corridor to tidewater either north or south lacks such evidence.

Taking into account these energy constraints, the adverse gradient and the absence of evidence of passage of a torrential flood along the routes to the sea, an interpretation of the 26,000-year Calgary "event" as a great lake release like Bonneville must be considered unlikely.

The remaining alternative is a catastrophic outburst of glacially entrapped water, a "jökuhlaup." These features have been much studied in Iceland, where volcanic heat under a glacier creates a water reservoir, which is held at first by the downstream segment of the glacier and then breaks out catastrophically.

If the continental ice and montane ice had bridged the ice-free corridor temporarily, it is not hard to imagine ponding of all runoff north of Calgary. This could have provided a reservoir of sufficient water for the 4 000 000 m³/s (3,200 ac-ft/s) brief and sudden catastrophic south-directed surge needed to produce the cataform Glenmore stratum.

Catastrophic failure of an ice dam has been exhaustively treated by Waitt (1986) in connection with Lake Missoula. His conclusion will be discussed in subsequent pages. The mechanism appears capable of producing the features of the Glenmore stratum and is certainly more appropriate than a surge from tidewater [as I proposed in 1977].

One problem remains, however: the charcoal distribution in the silt. There is no basis for expecting charcoal from a glacial outburst. A forest conflagration is implied by the charcoal. The association of heat with torrential flooding points directly to a comet for the explanation. Cometary melting of glacial ice could result in massive and rapid water production. And, in the absence of local volcanism, only a comet would have the incendiary capability needed to create a general conflagration and simultaneously to precipitate a great flood.

Exigency for a comet as precursor to the Calgary flood of 26,000 yBP, for melting glacial ice and setting forests ablaze, is unavoidable.

Drumlinfields: Fluvial Cataforms

In September, 1989, as this book was reaching final form, a study of drumlins in northern Saskatchewan and Ontario by John Shaw of Queens University brought new light to the subject of under-ice water discharge. Drumlins are mounds of fluvially-deposited, sometimes-stratified, sand and gravel which in some cases may have been moulded after deposition by overriding glacial ice.

Shaw observed, as have others including me, that huge fields of these features occur. The drumlins are found side by side in fields 50 km in width and length, with 50 m heights and 1 to 2-km lengths and parallel orientation so perfect that only a massive water flow could have produced them (Photo scene 12). Shaw concludes after exhaustive field study *as I had concluded after less direct study* that these drumlins are not glacial but fluvial deposition.

"Glacigenetic" is the currently favored term to describe deposits of glacier-related agencies, in this case, under-ice water flow. I had previously decided not to include discussion of drumlins in this book because of my own insufficient direct work on them. Shaw has done the work I would like to have done; and he has drawn the appropriate major conclusions: **Discharge of 84 000 km³ of water at 3.6 km³/hr over a flow path 60-150 km in width.**

Shaw's work was in northern Saskatchewan and southern Ontario. Drumlinfields of this sort occur elsewhere. My observations in northern Alberta and northeastern British Columbia led me to consider the drumlins I observed on air photographs as fluvial features because of their regularity in orientation, spacing and length, the same characteristics attributed by Shaw to flood deposition.

Shaw emphasizes that catastrophic floodwater release is an

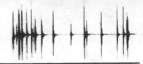

SCENE 12

A DRUMLINFIELD IN NORTHEASTERN ALBERTA

Drumlins and flutings that comprise a drumlinfield are respectively features of deposition and excavation of Pleistocene age. Their lengths are 1-2 km, their widths, 100 m or so.

inescapable conclusion. He also recognizes likelihood for such releases from *other* sides of the continental glacier than the south side, where his studies occurred. No doubt one would find drumlinfields in northern and eastern Canada as well. These occurrences, if generated simultaneously with those known to Shaw and me, will multiply the overall cataform by at least an order of magnitude.

Curiously, Shaw does not contemplate (in print, at any rate) where the water could have originated, apparently assuming it to be sub-glacial meltwater. But how could such melting take place without a heat source such as the volcanic heat, which precipitates Icelandic jökulhaups? What climatic regimen would allow such melting in the first place? Why would the water not have lifted the periphery of the ice sheet and emerged without accumulating soon after it was produced by melting? What containment mechanism would allow accumulation of a great under-ice lake, 84 000 km^3 of water, *18 times the volume of the Bonneville flood release,* beneath 3 000 m of ice? And would not water

beneath the maximum ice thickness tend to escape toward the lesser confining pressures under peripheral areas of the ice sheet? Is there any possible way such a huge under-ice chamber of water could accumulate?

Overlooking for the moment the apparent impossibility that a water volume such as Shaw's 84 000 km³ could ever accumulate under an unconfined ice sheet, and assuming it did burst out as Shaw imagines, what must have been the behavior of the glacier itself?

Ice has no effective tensile strength. Thus, **any unconstrained portion of an ice sheet above a moving torrent would move with the water, breaking up and flowing as icebergs with it. Any rock load that might be encased in the ice would go with the flood. Catastrophic emergence of floodwaters from under an ice sheet would rapidly destroy the ice sheet.**

Floating of the glacier was the thesis I advanced in my 1977 paper, "Catastrophic termination of the last Wisconsin ice advance". Shaw's deductions serve to reinforce my advocacy of that concept.

Earth heat cannot have melted continental ice to produce floodwaters in the volumes required for drumlinfield formation. A cometary heat source could have served the purpose. If we multiply Shaw's flood by ten to account for flow outward in all directions, 840 000 km³ of ice, or about ten percent of the Wisconsin glacier, would have had to melt. This melting would have required about 67×10^{23} calories, a caloric value that could have been obtained from conversion of the kinetic energy of a 500-m projectile with a specific gravity of 2.1 and travelling at the commonplace speed of 20 000 km/s.

A comet of the type that exploded above the Tunguska site in 1908 could have provided this heat. The great lake it might have created in the middle of the ice sheet would rapidly have tunnelled under the remaining glacier and emerged as catastrophic floods in many directions. Cometary melting of the ice seems necessary to yield so much water in such a short time.

The reader will remember that in the Tunguska "event" no crater form was left on the ground. Neither was an ejecta blanket formed. In the 11,000-years-ago terminal Wisconsin "event" in

Canada all ejecta and cometary matter would likely have been swept away in the ensuing "flood", coming to rest widely dispersed in the "drift" blanket far from its source. Thus diluted and mixed with other debris, direct evidence for either the exploded projectile or ejecta from the impact site could be difficult to recognize, if not lost to science permanently.

Glass spherules, if found in glacial debris, could be taken to support the theory. Glass and pseudotachylite impregnating a basement crater-form would also be indicative. Needless to say, neither is known at present. Search for these objectives in connection with crater forms of youthful nature on the Canadian Shield might produce interesting results. But the facts do not encourage the idea that such evidence ever was produced or, if produced, that it will have been preserved.

The Lake Missoula (Spokane) Flood

Lake Missoula was an enormous Pleistocene lake centering near Missoula, Montana, in the drainage of the Clark Fork River, a tributary of the Columbia in eastern Washington and Idaho. The lake was first described by Pardee (1910).

Many cataform features of the floodplain of this lake were first discovered and explained to an incredulous and unreceptive geological community by J. Harlan Bretz in 1919. Prevalent antipathy to catastrophic theories was sufficient that Bretz only gained marginal acceptance even after forty years of advocacy. General acceptance did not come for sixty years, just before his death in the 1980s.

Discharges of the waters of Lake Missoula over the "channelled scabland" (Photo scene *13*) of eastern Washington sculpted that distinctive terrane, which itself is the most impressive cataform feature. Bretz shows that sheet runoff was needed for such scouring.

The former bottom of Lake Missoula exhibits large transverse ridges. Pardee in 1942 called them "giant ripple marks" attributable to large-scale hydraulic movements of the released lake. The

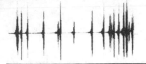

CHANNELLED SCABLAND
Near Ewan, Washington

SCENE 13

lake bottom is also host to "matrix-supported cobbles and boulders ... which are overlain with massive very fine unvarved silt" (Curry), a description that sounds just like the Calgary Silt.

"The" Lake Missoula torrential flood, as it was called for some time, deposited rhythmically layered silt and sand in lateral canyons of the Columbia system through which its waters discharged [Waitt]. These "rhythmites", as they are called, were sedimentary remnants of eddies backwashing into lateral tributaries along the course of the main floods. Forty or more in number, the rhythmites were deposited at 10- to 70-year intervals, each rhythmite attesting to one of Missoula's catastrophic lake releases.

The rhythmite evidence from the flood course is consistent with the beach evidence from the lake basin. Weakly developed beaches indicative of short-lived stands of lake level are found rimming the Lake Missoula basin. The highly variable levels of these numerous, persistent and immature beach features imply releases *not* as a function of a persistent spillway level but as the result of an irregular function such as glacial outburst.

The foregoing describes generally accepted late Pleistocene events at Lake Missoula in the period, 15,000-12,800 years ago (Allen's dates). Curry deduces from caliche thicknesses of earlier deposits in the Lake Missoula basin that "there were [earlier] catastrophic lake drainings ... [as early as] 200,000 to 300,000 years ago."

In addition to the aforesaid features, the discharges of Lake Missoula produced great mounded gravel bars on the eastern Washington "scablands" and ice-rafted erratics as far downstream as the Willamette Valley of northwestern Oregon. These will come up again in connection with Erratics.

Lake Pend Oreille: The "Ice Dam'"

Pend Oreille Lake received the aforesaid forty or more discharges of Lake Missoula. The 300-m-deep lake occupies a depression in the north-south "Purcell trench", a structural depression separating mature topography of the Selkirk Range on the west from more youthful topography of the Purcell and Cabinet Ranges on the east.

The basin of Lake Pend Oreille and its Miocene predecessor, "Rathdrum Lake", is an Eocene trough cut into crystalline rocks and later filled in by Cenozoic sedimentation. The Lake defined local base level. It appears to have been near sea level throughout Cenozoic time. Pleistocene erosion and glaciation must have developed the Purcell and Cabinet Range scenery when its elevation was 500 m or so lower than at present.

Glacial ice is considered to have surged south in the Purcell trench damming the Clark Fork River, which drained Lake Missoula. The ice dam in time was floated *forty or more times* by rising lake water, which then discharged under and around the ice. Turbulence of the underflow eroded Cenozoic bottom sediment, thus deepening Lake Pend Oreille.

The final discharge, marking the Pleistocene/Holocene transition, removed the load of water and ice from the terrain and may have allowed terrain rebound and uplift, thus enhancing the

scenery of the "youthful" terrain east of the Purcell trench to its present majesty.

Ice Dams: Lakes Calgary and Missoula

The Calgary ice-free corridor as an impoundment basin compares with Lake Missoula in area and altitude. The elevation of the Lake Missoula surface was the same as the highest ice-rafted Erratics of the Calgary corridor, and it was about 650 m (2,100 ft) above its debouchment on Lake Pend Oreille.

The proposition before us is that river flow from Lake Missoula was impounded by ice surging south across the course of the Clark Fork River and damming its course where the River emerged from the Cabinet Range. Generally accepted today, this concept has aspects that I find difficult to believe.

How, one must ask, could an ice dam be made to hold against hydrostatic pressure of more than 64 kg/cm² (910 psi)? Concrete dams of one-third the height require bedrock grouting to avoid being bypassed by water. Would not an ice dam be equally susceptible to failure in this manner? And, at the same time, would it not be less competent to withstand the pressure? Waitt's analysis considers only barrier bouyancy while ignoring ice incompetence and the high likelihood of bedrock by-passing. I think it not unreasonable to propose that the highly-pressured impounded waters would have burrowed and seeped under and around the ice dam, thus disrupting it before it had impounded water to depths of 650 m.

The idea may be advanced that the glacier would have frozen the ground and prevented by-passing in that way. Freezing of the shaft walls in deep mines is commonplace today, where water pressures compare to those of Lake Missoula's hypothetical ice dam. For this to have happened at Lake Missoula would have required Arctic cold *in the ice at the contact*. That would require still greater cold in the glacial environment, a condition that is not thought to have prevailed. If it had, there could have been no water flow at all either in the river or under the glacier.

Whether these concerns are the only ones critical to the problem is not known. Our knowledge of the ability of a continental ice sheet to make an ice dam in a temperate climate is non-existent.

The Elevation Factor: Calgary/Missoula/Bonneville

Because I am uneasy over the feasibility of the ice dam concept for Lake Missoula, I propose that dilation of the entire terrain from Calgary to Missoula has occurred in the 11,000 years since the end of Wisconsin time. This process may have been one of terrain rebound after depression under the load of Pleistocene ice and water. In any case, the existence of youthful terrain in the Lake Missoula area is supportive of the idea that it has been raised recently relative to the Lake Pend Oreille trough.

The top beach levels of Lake Missoula as well as the highest Alberta Erratics indicate lake water levels on the present topography of about 1 400 m (4,200 ft) above sea level. Recent uplift of the Calgary area as well as the mountainous terrain from Calgary to Missoula, but not of Lake Pend Oreille, makes the concept of ice damming of Lake Missoula look more feasible to me. I propose that the extremely high apparent lake surface elevations of both lakes, Missoula and Calgary, are illusions resulting from terrain rebound of the last 11,000 years.

Terrain depression brought on by a short-lived immense buildup of ice is a real possibility that could have depressed the land surface. Farther south, Lake Bonneville experienced terrain elevation changes in the same period, with cataclysmic consequences. Discussion is deferred to allow a description of the Bonneville terrain and circumstances, which follow next.

Lake Bonneville: Early Work, Current Doctrine

Lake Bonneville is the Pleistocene ancestral name of the huge body of water that occupied the basin in which Great Salt Lake

survives today. The Lake surface area in Pliocene and Pleistocene times was 51 530 km², nine times the 5 700 km² area of Great Salt Lake. G. K. Gilbert investigated the region for the U.S. Geological Survey in 1875-80 and developed concepts of lake origin, which prevail to this day. There is reason to question some aspects of this doctrine.

The essentials of current ideas are that the lake basin filled to overflow level at the Bonneville beach elevation, which then was well above present Red Rock Pass outlet elevation (1 500 m). At about 30,000 years BP the lake overflowed, breaching its "outlet" lip and draining away a volume of water comprising its basin volume between the Bonneville and Provo beach levels, a volume of 4 700 km³ (Jarratt & Malde). Subsequently, the lake has evaporated under changed climatic conditions to its present Great Salt Lake remnant. Recent climate is thought to be more desertic than Pleistocene climate, which was thought to have provided the basin more precipitation.

The waters that drained off, when the "outlet" was breached, passed to the sea through the Snake and lower Columbia rivers. Water levels during "catastrophic release" have been mapped along the Snake River (Malde, and Jarratt & Malde). Estimates of flow volumes and velocity have thusly been calculated. As mentioned earlier, the maximum flow rate of 935 000 m³/s was calculated.

So far, so good. But is this the whole story? Gilbert's notebooks certainly support his reputed idea of

["a magnitude of the *outflowing stream* that is truly astounding" (Oct. 14, 1879, my italics, see C.B. Hunt, 1981).] But they do not stop with that simplistic outlook. For example, he speaks of ["the Bonneville River" which he perceived as "a large one that [had] excavated the great canyon [of Marsh Creek leading north to the Snake River]. Perhaps the great canyon was chiefly excavated before Bonneville [time], and the B. river merely cleared out the alluvium."

Thus, Gilbert recognized a large valley-cutting river *and* he recognized a catastrophic release. Gilbert persistently referred to the "Bonneville River" implying protracted erosion and alluvia-

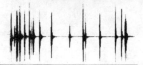

tion over much greater time than has elapsed since development of the Bonneville beaches. The implied antiquity of terrain reveals that Gilbert held an entirely different outlook from the simplistic picture of catastrophic release as above described and attributed to him.

The fundamental problem with the popularly held, simplistic idea of outflow drainage cutting down Red Rock Pass shows clearly in the geomorphology. The landforms should show evidence supportive of the outflow, features apparent to a lay person. It does not take a geologist to recognize that erosional downcutting of a spillway from one level to a lower one must have created a *V-shaped gully on the Pass,* a gorge, which today should be highly visible.

What we find on Red Rock Pass is different. **The Pass is not V-shaped as it should be, but wide and flat-floored. Its 16-km length is flanked by low depositional terraces made up of fine clastic materials characteristic of quiescent deposition.**

A further feature that one would look for in any vigorous fluvial process is impact-polishing and scouring of channel walls. Entrained sand and gravel act as cutting agents to scour and polish such obstacles. The resulting impacted and polished rock surfaces should be visible today.

What I have found in a gravel excavation just east of the two-lane highway precisely on the Pass is most revealing - a **polished vertical rock surface facing north. Turbulent water has flowed south past this obstacle, across the Pass and *into* Lake Bonneville. No comparable south-facing rock face demonstrates northward flow.** (Photo scene *14*).

Malde estimates the age of the "catastrophic flood" that was released northward out of Pleistocene Lake Bonneville at 30,000 yBP. I will refer to it arbitrarily as the 26,000 yBP "event" or flood because its date is so close to that of the Calgary Silt as to suggest contemporaneity and because my radiocarbon date looks more precise than Malde's estimates.

The period after 26,000 yBP until 11,000 yBP, when Provo Beach development ended, does not seem long enough for flow in any direction to have excavated the great canyon of Marsh Creek. Gilbert implied as much. The great canyon is undoubtedly due to

SCENE 14

RED ROCK PASS

Above: Bonneville River valley looking north from Red Rock Pass.

Right: Water-worn and polished bed-rock surface looking south, showing southward flow of Bonneville River. Site is immediately east of high point on highway over Pass. The rock surface has been exposed by extraction of gravel talus that had covered it, for road building use

BLACK ROCK DESERT
Northwestern Nevada

The mid-trunk of a giant ceder [or redwood], 3m (8′) diameter as it stood before interment in tephra in late Pleistocene time. The bark and outer layer of wood are petrified in porcellanous cream-white silica. The inner trunk is weathered away and the shaft open 10m down. Desert dust would have filled the void if its age were greater than late Pleistocene.

Tertiary or earlier fluviation. Let us review what is known of the local Tertiary record.

Lake Bonneville: Perspectives over Geological Time

A Cretaceous and Paleocene record is lacking at Lake Bonneville. It is thought the area was emergent (above sea level), drainage generally being eastward into the mid-continental seaway, which had long connected the Gulf of Mexico with the Arctic Ocean. The seaway was increasingly becoming restricted in this period.

Eocene time was one of greater emergence and saw deposition of a thick sequence of subaerial clastics, the Wasatch group (recognized and named by Hayden, 1869). Valley fills of conglomerate from this period were laid in eastward-draining valleys crossing the "Wasatch" line (Plate I). This is the position of the present crest of the Wasatch Mountains, where the Wasatch deposits are preserved today. The strata become progressively finer eastward, showing that they arrived from the west. The Eocene river that carried them emptied into great freshwater lakes of the Green River basin. At about the end of Eocene time the rise of the Colorado Plateau and of the Wasatch Mountains reversed the drainage to westward and perched the old Green River basin high above its former elevation.

Thus, passes across the rising Wasatch range were the course of rivers *from* the west. Weber River and Echo Creek were east-flowing before becoming choked with as much as 770 m of conglomeratic clastics. Today these water courses conduct flow *toward* the west, the reversed interior drainage system of the Great Basin in western Utah, which still prevails today.

The subsidence that much later became the Bonneville basin was deepened in Oligocene time and extended to tidewater on the Gulf of California to the southwest. This is known from the fact that nearly 2 000 m of salt with oceanic ion balance was deposited during Oligocene time in the Sevier desert depression of southwestern Utah (Mitchell, 1979).

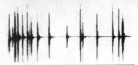

Miocene through early Pliocene paleogeography of adjacent Great Basin terrains in Utah, Nevada, Idaho, and Oregon was characterized by interior drainage and warm desertic conditions. A great lake system known as the "Humboldt Lakes" (Stokes, 1979) occupied northeast Nevada and northwest Utah. **Its meteoric water was supplied through the southward-flowing Bonneville River from the terrain of today's eastern Snake River watershed.**

In middle Pliocene time isostatic readjustments modified the interior drainage of the Humboldt system creating lakes, Lahontan in Nevada, Idaho in Idaho and Oregon, and Bonneville in Utah.

Wheeler and Cook (1954) proposed that in Miocene time the Snake River flowed through southwestern Idaho and Oregon into western Nevada and thence down the Feather River system of northern California to the embayment that comprised the Great Valley at that time. They proposed that southward drainage from Lake Idaho continued until interrupted by capture of Snake drainage by headward encroachment of the Columbia system at Oxbow on the Idaho-Oregon border.

Whereas Wheeler and Cook thought of capture as a Pliocene occurrence, I suggest that the appearance of the Oxbow "capture site" and other factors imply a more complex and very much more lengthy history.

All Cenozoic lakes of the Great Basin had low altitudes in my opinion. Thus, the Miocene outpouring of Columbia basalts easily obstructed the Snake, as Wheeler and Cook suggest, and caused backing up of the Salmon River to flow south through Hell's Canyon into Lake Idaho and thence through the basin of the future great lake of Nevada, Lake Lahontan, to California. Meanwhile, the upper Snake was feeding Humboldt Lake, as previously mentioned.

In the Black Rock Desert of northwestern Nevada forests of immense trees grew on the shores of Pleistocene Lake Lahontan. The trees must be of that youthful age because their trunk cavities would have collapsed or filled with wind-blown silt ("loess") if any older. I interpret their age as 10,000 to 15,000 years on this basis. (Photo scene 15).

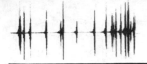

By the same reasoning a life-giving southward water flow would have been essential to sustain both the great desert lake and the humidity required for floral verdure. I suggest that the giant cedar (or redwood) forest, which once thrived in this sagebrush desert of northern Nevada, is mute testimony that Snake River waters continued to supply the region until approximately 11,000 yBP. Thus, it is likely the Snake did not resume flow into the Columbia system until the southward flow ceased and the desiccation of Lake Lahonton had commenced. This theory better explains the sustained high level of Lake Lahontan than the dubious idea that the Pleistocene was a time of much increased rainfall.

With this background we are in position to consider again the flows of water across Red Rock Pass and through the great canyon of Marsh Creek. The conglomerates of the Eocene Wasatch group as found on Weber River are obvious candidates for excavation products of the great canyon of Marsh Creek. Southward flow of Gilbert's "Bonneville River" also explains the otherwise-enigmatic Red Rock Pass landforms.

Only 168 m (550 ft) of elevation today separates Red Rock Pass and the Snake River at Pocatello, a difference which may reflect either differential rebound or terrain dilation after 11,000 yBP. Recent rebound/dilation, of course, ties in well with that already suggested for the terrain of lakes Missoula and Calgary.

Southward and thence eastward water flow from the eastern Snake basin, which commenced through a lower-elevation Red Rock Pass in Eocene time, continued until Quaternary time. It provided water for the Humboldt Lakes of the Miocene and early Pliocene and for Lake Bonneville of later Pliocene and Pleistocene times.

The inflow to Lake Bonneville was well established in Pleistocene time and the channel aggraded, perhaps even pro-graded with deltaic fill as Gilbert surmised. I propose that the water release was not an overflowing down-cutting process as current belief requires, but a "decantation event". Rapid uplift at about 26,000 yBP, with tilting of the entire Bonneville basin is the simplest scenario to fit the facts.

Southward flow of the "Bonneville River" was reversed by lake basin rise. Water and boulders were discharged past Pocatello into

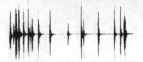

American Falls Lake, a 40-m-deep lake that occupied the Snake plain for 50 km southwest and 20 km northeast of Pocatello. Its lava containment barrier was short lived. The flood rapidly overtopped it, and waters of the upper Snake River basin, perhaps for the first time, were established on a westward course into Lake Idaho.

The uplift that caused decantation of Lake Bonneville and backup of "Bonneville River" must have been sudden and powerful because boulder terraces with clasts up to 7 m in diameter were carried in the torrent (the "Michaud Gravels"). They were left lining the flow path westward from Pocatello, where they rest on fine-grained lake deposits of American Falls Lake. They are associated with fossils having carbon dates that cluster near 26,000 yBP (Scott et al, 1982). Despite the absence of younger carbon dates in the flood deposits, Scott et al discount the age data as spurious, suggesting instead that the samples are "re-worked materials".

I demur on many detailed grounds. My major objection, however, is that the beaches of the "Provo" level [the Red Rock Pass spillway elevation] required much time for their development. These beaches are cut deeply into the hillsides of the Bonneville basin and in places are represented by huge aprons and wave-shaped longshore bars of sand, shingle, and shoreline debris. Their mature condition, and the fact that they had to have been built *after* the Bonneville flood, make 15,000 years (from 26,000 to 11,000 yBP) for their development look reasonable.

If the Bonneville flood opened the 15,000-year period of Provo time with a deluge that overtopped the American Falls barrier; its start must have been either a drop in the level of Red Rock Pass or a rise of the Bonneville Lake basin, or a combination of the two. If dilation of the Bonneville basin had been accompanied by an earthquake, as seems likely, it is easy to visualize a tsunami wave in Lake Bonneville as Malde suggests. Overtopping Red Rock Pass the catastrophic flood continued for a few weeks during which 4 700 km³ of water were decanted.

The Snake plain is a subsident trough, the surface of which exhibits relict beach ridges for 125 km north from Pocatello in which only a 100-m rise in elevation occurs. The waters from the

surrounding mountains ponded in late Tertiary and Quaternary time in the Pocatello area, making American Falls Lake. The accumulated waters flowed south through Marsh Creek, Gilbert's "great canyon of the Bonneville River" into Lake Bonneville.

The basin of the upper Snake River plain is a natural basin because of subsidence, not river erosion. Mapping in the Pocatello area by Trimble and Carr (1961) and Scott et al (1982) establishes no evidence of river flow westward past Pocatello before the Bonneville "flood" overtopped the American Falls Lake containment barrier near American Falls. West of that barrier they describe lake sediments (Raft River strata) on the floor of the valley as clastics of quiescent fluviatile and lacustrine deposition.

The Trimble and Carr report offers no obstacle to the theory here advanced, that up to the time of the Bonneville "flood" the upper Snake basin was drained by a southward-flowing Bonneville River.

We should now return to the "flood" event on Red Rock Pass. Malde considered that the flood release was triggered by a catastrophic "event". This "event", he theorized, resulted from capture of Lake Thatcher by the Bear River, which released its waters directly into Lake Bonneville. Lake Thatcher formerly drained west into American Falls Lake, the source area of Bonneville River. The sudden surge of water from Bear River into Lake Bonneville, Malde thought, could have caused the breaching of the Red Rock Pass barrier.

My analysis can accommodate the Lake Thatcher/Bear River capture but not the down-cutting of the Pass through alluvial fill. There is no sign that the Pass was a barrier at any time to water flow north or south above Provo level. I am unable to find any evidence whatsoever to justify concurrence with either Gilbert or Malde that significant alluvial fill ever blocked Red Rock Pass.

I aver that the best fit to the facts is an interpretation of a series of events of uplift and depression of the Lake Bonneville basin and Red Rock Pass terrain. These allowed water flows as shown in the geomorphology. I interpret the occurrence of paroxysmal uplift in the 26,000-year "event" that raised the lake level from an elevation of about 1 300 m to about 1 400 m, just enough to allow

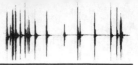

the "flood" as a great decantation "event". After the paroxysm and draining off of 4 700 km³ of lake water, I interpret that subsidence (below present level) of the Bonneville basin reestablished itself, and water flow south into the lake continued for the next 15,000 years, during which time prominent Provo shorelines were notched into the walls of the Bonneville basin.

The evidence for the outflowing Bonneville "flood" *on Red Rock Pass is not visible today because resumed inflow has aggraded the Pass with later deposition.* In any case, it must be recognized that the discharge waters of the Bonneville flood were moving at their minimal velocity on the Pass. Their torrential behavior developed as they descended Marsh Creek Valley and passed Pocatello. Erosion during the brief outflow episode was easily obscured by the subsequent 15,000 years of inflow to Lake Bonneville. The low terraces along the course of Bonneville River on the Pass as well as the beaches of the Provo level are the products of the 15,000-year Provo period. They were created entirely after the "flood" and before inflow was terminated abruptly by uplift of the Pass area 11,000 years ago.

Desiccation of the Lahontan basin as well as of the Bonneville basin likely occurred only after 11,000 yBP. Contrary to current belief, the Bonneville flood of 26,000 years ago did not initiate this desiccation. Water from Idaho flowed into both basins and was not finally terminated until Holocene time, when uplift of the terrain of the feeder rivers stopped the flows.

The 26,000 yBP Bonneville flood "event" was not a case of downcutting of the rim of the lake at Red Rock Pass so much as a decantation of the lake due to dilation of the lake terrain. After decantation, subsidence followed and southward waterflow resumed. A second stage of elevation of the Pass terrain finally ended inflow at 11,000 yBP, the start of Holocene times.

To this point our discussion has dealt only with the Pass area, where direct "flood" evidence for outflowing water is absent and, in its place one observes relics of quiescent southward river flow. Reinterpretation of the evidence from this area does not, however, portend similar reinterpretation downstream on the Snake River.

There, the situation is different. Great boulder aprons and

perched remnants of highly rounded boulders up to five metres in diameter testify to passage of enormous flood volumes. These occurrences have been reported exhaustively by Jarratt and Malde (Photo scene 16), whose engineering interpretation of the hydrology of a flood "event" is considered competent and not a subject of dispute here. But it should give the reader pause to note that these authors do not tackle the Pass geology in any significant way while performing precise calculations on down-river aspects of the same "event."

If the theory is right farther down the River; it should be right on the Pass, where landforms are not explainable by any form of barrier-breaching catastrophic release. These facets of the geological montage of Lake Bonneville demand treatment within any acceptable theory of origin and history. The essentials that have not been recognized by other analysts of the problem are: southward "inflow" and lower elevation of the Bonneville basin than the Snake River plain.

Still farther down the Snake River, beyond Malde's study area, the Tammany Creek section at Lewiston, Idaho, exposes a bevelled foreset series of Bonneville flood gravels overlain by a thick flat-lying deposit of Missoula graded silt representing back-flood deposition up the Snake River. The exposures elegantly illustrate the age sequence, the Missoula being younger than the Bonneville.

The flow of the Bonneville flood through the Snake River into the Columbia was, according to Wheeler and Cook, a barrier-topping "event" similar to its barrier-topping at American Falls. My information is insufficient to address that subject more fully than the suggestion that after passage of the flood, Lake Idaho water still found its way southward to Lake Lahontan, a situation that prevailed until Recent times.

Lake Bonneville: A Summary

Bonneville River in Eocene time was a vigorous southward-flowing river that eroded the great canyon of today's Marsh Creek. Fluviation was southward and thence eastward across

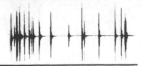

SCENE 16

BONNEVILLE BOULDERS

Above: Typical boulder fan, near Bliss dam, southcentral Idaho. Boulders appear too much rounded for rounding to have occurred in the short transit from the canyon at Twin Falls. More likely, many of them were rounded earlier by river action and then were flushed en masse out of the canyon by the Flood.

Below: The Bonneville Flood excavated channels like these into floodplain deposits earlier laid down by the Snake River.

the "Wasatch line" into freshwater Lakes Goshute and Uinta of the Green River basin of eastern Utah, Wyoming and Colorado.

In late Eocene time the Wasatch mountains rose, blocking the eastward flow. The continued southward flow of Bonneville River in Oligocene time was carried across western Utah in a depression connected to the Gulf of California. Obstacles along this waterway caused Oligocene salt deposition in the Sevier basin, the south limb of future Lake Bonneville.

Humboldt Lake occupied northwestern Utah and northeastern Nevada in Miocene time and repositioned itself into Pliocene Lake Bonneville, which was sustained until 11,000 yBP. Continuous southward river flow over 40 million years was interrupted only briefly by the "Bonneville flood event" of about 26,000 yBP which allowed decantation of 4 700 km³ of lakewater northward into the Snake basin.

The torrent overwhelmed American Falls Lake at Pocatello, overflowing its containment barrier, and raged westward 500 km or so into the Lake Idaho basin. That lake had been draining southward into Lake Lahontan. The Bonneville water caused Lake Idaho to overflow its northern barrier into Columbia River drainage.

General terrain dilation of the Bonneville basin has occurred from 11,000 yBP (200 m or about 2 cm/yr). In addition, the central part of the Great Salt Lake basin is rebounding in domal fashion (Charles B. Hunt, 1981),

ERRATICS

The point of departure for any analysis of erratics in western North America is appropriately the herculean trail of rock known as the Alberta Erratics Train. Its largest member, the "Big Rock" at Okotoks, weighted about 18 000 tonnes, and required a 160 000 m³ 5,500,000 ft³ iceberg to float it to its resting place on prairie farmland (Photo scene 17).

Quartzite boulders comprising the Alberta Erratics are strewn in a "train" 25 km or so in width along the foothills of the Rocky Mountains from the Athabaska River valley to the Sweetgrass Arch on the Montana border.

The rock is a Cambrian quartzite that occurs on a ridge near the headwaters of the Athabaska River south of the town of Jasper. The fresh, mountain-derived rock shows no effects from its 650-km journey.

Erratics Train: Ice Rafting

I proposed in 1977 that the "event" responsible for the Erratics Train also had the effect of terminating Wisconsin glaciation. The agency of termination, I surmised, was a disruptive flood. I proposed that an earthquake, perhaps caused by an exogenic event (a comet?), caused an avalanche of rock on top of the Athabaska Glacier. Flooding then floated the snout of the glacier off its basal moorings up to 1 300 m elevation. And the icebergs with their loads of rock ebbed with the tide along the ice-free corridor, beaching or otherwise dropping their rock loads along the way.

Since that proposal was made it has come to my attention (Sugden and John, 1976, p33) that just such an avalanche occurred in 1964 on the Sherman glacier, Alaska. An area of 8.5 km² was covered to a depth averaging 5 m.

Ice rafting of the Erratics is given support by the fact of concordant maximal elevations of deposition of the Erratics along their route. This top elevation for the ebbing tide is about 1 300 m, or 400 m above the Calgary topography. The ice rafts must have floated, then, at a level 250 m above the assumed Calgary Silt flood depth.

Ice rafting is supported strongly by the character of the rock, which is fresh and not water- or ice-worn. Lacking signs of glacial mauling such as striations, chattermarks or slicked surfaces precludes the interpretation of this rock having been ingested into a glacial interior.

The problem of where sufficient water for ice-rafting might have originated has three possible answers: tidewater inundation, glacier surge damming with catastrophic outbursting, and sudden cometary glacier melting. The first could originate with depres-

THE OKOTOKS ERRATIC   SCENE 17
The "big rock" with many fragments falling from it.
Note a smaller erratic in the foreground of the upper frame.

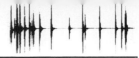

This is fresh Cambrian quartzite from a mountain source above the Athabaska River south of Jasper townsite, Alberta. The fresh rock character shows well in these closeup photographs. Lack of glacial striae or chattermarks discredits delivery by glacier. The Rocky Mountain skyline is visible in the background.

SCENE 17

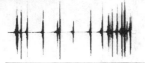
sion of the land surface or from a tsunami. The second could result from glacial surge across the ice-free corridor in the manner of the Lake Missoula ice damming. The third could ensue from any comet impact.

The sheer volume of the flood impels one to choose between the more catastrophic first and third scenarios. The ice dam competence problem militates against the second. The Erratics lack a charcoal association, but they have the probable drumlin-fields association to imply a probable cometary solution. The tidewater solution is weakened by the great distance to tidewater and the absence of a trail of evidence along the possible routes.

Erratics Train: Glacier Delivery

Notwithstanding the evidence favoring ice-rafting, some Quaternary geologists still support glacial delivery of the Erratics. Glacial delivery appears impossible to me for several reasons.

The first of these is the net uphill gradient ($+100$ m) from the point of emergence of the Athabasca glacier from the mountains (near Hinton, Alberta) where it turns south toward Calgary and the point of passage over the Sweetgrass Arch near Coutts, Alberta.

The second objection is the multiplicity of valleys comprising the undulating course of the "ice-free corridor." Each of these would present a major obstacle to southward ice flow.

The third objection to the glacial delivery mechanism is that the ice-free nature of the corridor [and its raison d'être] would disappear. The corridor would become ice-clogged as soon as the monster glacier "galloped" into it.

The fourth serious objection I have to a glacial delivery mechanism for the Alberta Erratics is that prominent lateral moraines would be expected to mark the course of such a glacier. Such features are absent; and their absence cannot be attributed to later destruction by glacial action, as the Erratics "event" is conceded by all to be the last Wisconsin activity.

What validity do these objections have? Firstly, at the aforesaid

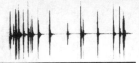
right turn near Hinton on the Athabaska River, a towering [and absurd] 7-km-high ice surface would be necessary to drive the glacial snout southward as far as Coutts. This is based on the .7° top slope measured on the 200-km Bering glacier. That glacier advances about 3 km/year. Thus, the Erratics Train glacier with those characteristics would require more than 200 years to deliver the farthest fraction of Erratics across the U.S. border.

The second problem, successive interfluves, is also not inconsequential. After making its right-angle turn near Hinton, Alberta, the ice would need to surmount nineteen successive interfluves, many of them with 300 metres of relief. If a glacier progressed over these obstacles the valleys between them would become choked with stagnant ice, thus aggravating the third problem.

A glacier filling the slot comprising the "ice-free corridor" for 200 years would block a lot of runoff otherwise handled by the corridor. Ponding of all the water shed from a 650-km length of the eastern slopes of the Rockies for even a few years, much less 200 years, would seem nearly impossible.

What, in fact, would happen is that the water would float the glacier sooner or later depending on temperatures. As moderate temperatures are thought to have prevailed, the concept of glacial delivery is not feasible because of the water factor alone.

A better option emerges from considering the water problem. If glacial ice surged from either side of the corridor so as to block it, the water buildup behind the ice dam would create conditions for flotation of the glacier and a catastrophic glacial outburst, a jökulhlaup, *providing the glacial surge snout had competence to dam the water to depths of 600 m.* If the damming could occur, ice-rafting could ensue naturally, as I first proposed, within the corridor.

The first root problem is insufficient gradient. This leads to the absurdity of a 7-km glacier surface height at Hinton, higher than the elevation of the original Erratics rock source.

The second root problem is the ability of a glacier in the ice-free corridor to surmount its grandly crenulated fluve/interfluve surface.

The third root problem, as mentioned already, is the absence of anywhere for the natural surface runoff to go while the glacier does its work.

Thus, if climate is moderate, ice and water, glaciers and ice rafts should work together toward movement of rock down the "ice-free corridor". On balance, the sheer volume of water should prove to be the more powerful mechanism. Glaciers alone for delivery of the Alberta Erratics appear wholly inadequate. Considered along with the absence of moraines or other positive evidence to demonstrate the existence of a glacier in the ice-free corridor, the concept of glacier delivery is too feeble to deserve further attention.

Erratics and Calgary Silt Ages

It was my belief in 1977 that the Calgary Silt comprised the waterborne component of the Erratics Train tidal flood. The apparent synchroneity of the Calgary "event" with the supposed Lake Bonneville outflow suggested a common origin.

The 26,000 yBP Silt date and Malde's revision of the Bonneville Flood date (to 30,000 yBP) negate my 1977 interpretation of synchroneity among Silt, the Bonneville Flood, and the 11,000 yBP Erratics. Effective contemporaneity still exists between the Silt and Bonneville events. I am using my 26,000-year figure for both.

Erratics of the Columbia/Fraser System

Exotic boulders weighing up to 160 tons and composed variously of pegmatitic kyanite, granite, gneiss, quartzite, and schist have been found in the Willamette Valley south of Portland, Oregon. Others are found along the walls of the gorge of the Columbia River and some have been rafted into tributaries as far as 16 km and up to elevations of 300 metres above river level.

The kyanite is identified by Allen as originating near Rev-

elstoke, British Columbia, and other clasts are also typical of the upper Columbia terrane. These boulders have been glacier-carried an unknown distance down the Columbia and then ice-rafted on bergs of glacial ice by the discharges of Lake Missoula. Again, as in the Alberta corridor, synergetic delivery by glacier and ice raft is recognizable.

Hydrodynamic Deposits

Getting into hyper-energy constructs leads to phenomena that are not understood in theory. Among these are great flow-oriented elongate ridges of mounded gravel reported long ago by Bretz on the channelled scablands of eastern Washington. Another such phenomenon is Pardee's "giant ripple marks" [previously mentioned] on the bottom surface of the Missoula floods.

The "mounds" have been current shaped, elongated in the direction of flow, up to kilometres in length and a hundred metres or so in height (Alt & Hyndman, 1989). The "ripple marks" in the fine clastics of the lake bottom are similar but for being transverse to flow direction. Both are regarded as products of unconfined massive flow, perhaps functions of the border conditions between chaotic action and ordered linear processes.

Flood-induced mounded gravels mimic glacier-oriented, if not glacier-produced drumlins. Geological interpretation of drumlins as glacial features and of mounded gravels as flood features appears to have been standard practice for the sole reason that a glacier was on hand for the former but not the latter. The premise of glacial involvement in the first place, being now recognizably false, the distinction should be dropped. All these features should be called drumlins, fluviatile deposits.

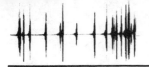

PART III

MAGNITUDES AND PERSPECTIVES ON CRATERS, DIAPIRS AND FLUVIAL CATAFORMS

The spectrum of cataforms presented in Parts I and II covering crater phenomena and fluvial features needs a scale by which various elements can be compared. The practice of comparing explosive events on the basis of energy release is not useful because most energy involved in cataform generation is dissipated without trace. Common features that can be measured or approximated in geology are magnitude of mass transferred and distance of movement.

With this in mind, mass transfers involved in ten cataforms from Parts I and II are calculated and organized in a table in which the indices of cataformity reflect quantitatively the extreme range of activity. Thus:

Index of   1-10 = Mag 1
Index of   10-100 = Mag 2
Index of   100-1,000 = Mag 3
Index of   1,000-10,000 = Mag 4
Index of   10,000-100,000 = Mag 5
Index of   100,000-1,000,000 = Mag 6
Index of   1,000,000-10,000,000 = Mag 7

The interpreted magnitude span, 1 - 6.9 for the ten cataforms, thus encompasses a ten-million-fold spectrum. The numbers are reproduced above so as to drive home the extent of this range.

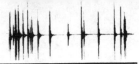

TABLE OF CATAFORM MAGNITUDES

	CATAFORM	MASS Km³	DENSITY Kg / Km³ x 10¹²	DISTANCE Km	INDEX KgxKm x 10¹⁵	ORDER OF Magnitude
	PRIMARY					
I	The "Alvarez" Crater, Hypothetical, K/T time	942 000	2.7	50	127 170	6.0
II	Proto-Mt. Shasta, J/K time Translation of Terrain	3 x 10⁶	2.7	100	810 000	6.9
III	Proto-Mt. Shasta, K/T time Conduit	50 000	2.8	50	7 000	4.8
	Lahars	600	2.5	80	120	3.0
IV	North American Strewnfield, Tektites	0.4	2.6	20 000	20.8	2.1
	Microtektites	14	2.6	20 000	728	3.8
V	Rocky Mountain Overthrusts	200 000	2.7	75	60 750	5.7
	SECONDARY					
VI	Saskatachewan Gravels, Boulder Broadcast	600	2.7	800	1 296	4.1
	Silt Component	352 000	.3	1 000	105 600	6.0
VII	Bonneville Flood, Silt Component	4 700	.3	1 550	2 185	4.1
	Boulders	2.4	2.5	169	1	1.0
VIII	Lake Missoula Flood, Silt Component	2 084	.3	750	469	3.6
IX	Lake Calgary Flood, Silt Component	624	.3	650	122	3.0
X	Alberta Erratica Train, Boulders	2.4x10⁻⁶	2.7	650	4.2x10⁻⁶	0.0
	Silt Component	5 000	.3	650	975	4.0

Some notes on each cataform follow:

I THE "ALVAREZ CRATER" 6.0 magnitude is the hypothetical 200-km astrobleme calculated to result from the impact of a 10-km-diameter bolide, which is thought to have been necessary for producing the worldwide K/T aerosol as recognized by Alvarez et al. No such crater has been found; its existence is in doubt. Entering it in this table is for perspective on comparative magnitudes.

Interpreted ejecta volume equals crater volume. It is assumed to be a 1-cm worldwide aerosol blanket, a 5 000 km³ volume included in the "boundary clay". The remaining 862 000 km³ is concomitant ejecta that is assumed to have been deposited within 50 km of the impact site. The 50-km travel distance may be too conservative. If so, the magnitude of the cataform is underestimated.

II THE PROTO-SHASTA scenario (from Part I) is given dimensions here. It is interesting to note the huge late Jurassic (Nevadan) magnitude 6.9 Klamath translation cataform that results from crustal inertia, nearly ten million times the Bonneville flood boulders standard (#VII).

III THE CRETACEOUS/TERTIARY WORLDWIDE AEROSOL, 4.8 magnitude, if delivered from an endogenic source, evidently might have been delivered with only 5% (7,000/127,170) of the total mass transfer of the imagined Alvarez impact event (#I).

IV THE NORTH AMERICAN TEKTITES had an estimated volume of one km^3 according to Glass; and the missive that caused them was quantized at 14 km^3 by Ganapathy. The report of the latter on microtektites, glass spherules, and associated siderophile metals in fallout from the late Eocene "event" is taken to mean that Ganapathy regards the fallout to be equatable to the size of the bolide. As much fallout could have been missed; and some ejecta may have left Earth's gravity influence, Ganapathy's result may be an underestimation but not an overestimation of the "event".

It is interesting that the tektite cataform at Magnitude *2.1* and the attendant microtektites at *3.8* are only two consequences of impact that caused them. The Caribou plateau gravels and accompanying silt are other cataforms that are probably of the same "event". Unfortunately, there is no data on which to base a direct estimation of magnitude for the Caribou plateau gravel cataform.

If we take the figures developed for the Saskatchewan Gravels, magnitudes *4.1* for gravel and **6.0** for its silt, we likely have figures comparable to those missing for the Caribou cataform. The sum of these indices **(6.04)** is the *apparent magnitude of cataformity,* and it should be a function of effective net energy investment in the geological features. Energy lost to space or dissipated to environment is geologically unmeasurable. Total magnitude, then is approximated by the 6.0 figure for the Saskatchewan Gravels silt fraction, as the addition of the other indices are inconsequential by comparison. The Caribou gravels may have been broadcast much farther if the wave front moved west from a Greenland impact site. Correcting for this would raise the 6.0 to a figure of perhaps *6.3* to *6.4*.

V THE ROCKY MOUNTAIN OVERTHRUSTS, magnitude 5.7 for the purposes here are taken as a 2 000-km length from Pine Pass of northeastern B.C. to the Green River basin of Utah and Colorado. The belt is taken to average 150 km in width and one km in depth. It is considered on average to be shortened into a 50 km width and 3 km depth.

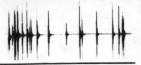

VI THE SASKATCHEWAN GRAVELS BOULDER BROADCAST, magnitude 6.0 must be viewed as an enormous cataform. The wave front that churned it up and carried it overland is assumed to have been 200 m deep. With 30% by weight of silt added to the water in the manner of the Calgary silt cataform, flood slurry density becomes 1.3. Deducting 1.0 for the water itself leaves a rock mass equivalent to three tenths of its water mass.

VII THE BONNEVILLE FLOOD, a hyper-energy event that is considerably more studied than others, is given perspective here using gravel and floodwater volumes taken from Malde, who calculated them at source and discharge levels. The highly visible boulderfields, surprisingly, turn out to give only a minor contribution to the grand cataform total, which manifestly must largely have been finer clastics.

The derived unit index figure for the much-studied boulders is an arithmetical coincidence. It conveniently provides a base for definition of the magnitude scale, which thusly acquired the *arbitrary Magnitude 1"*.

VIII THE LAKE MISSOULA FLOOD discharged at enormous rates because of *assumed elevation* difference between Lake Missoula and the Lake Pend Oreille debouchment terrain. Its boulder deposits have not been subjected to the amount of study or reporting given the Bonneville equivalent features. However, Bretz did call attention to large amounts of finer gravel and of a "mantle of silt" draped over everything, presumably final deposition. My interpretation assumes a slurry density of 1.3, as at Calgary.

Whereas my assumption of similarity between the Missoula and Calgary floods may seem a grand assumption that might be far from the mark, this concern fails if one considers that doubling of the index of cataformity raises the consequent magnitude only three tenths of a point.

Thus, the perspective derived from these magnitudes is not very sensitive to inaccuracies such as doublings or halvings of true values estimated for masses and distances of transport.

IX THE LAKE CALGARY FLOOD of 26,000 years ago laid down the archetypal silt and boulder cataform for the genre. Slurry density of 1.3 is assumed as a reasonable arbitrary value.

X THE ALBERTA ERRATICS TRAIN of 11,000 years age is overshadowed in magnitude when compared with the silt that must have accompanied it. The 11,000-year "event" has not yet been clearly shown to correlate with the drumlinfields. That *is* the implication, however, at least as to some drumlinfields. There may have been more than one period of drumlin generation.

The consequences of correlation of the drumlinfields with the Erratics Train "event" need to be considered. If we take the figure of 84 000 km³ water volume, which Shaw deduced for the drumlinfields he found, an interesting picture can be built. First we must multiply by ten to estimate runoff in all directions [Shaw only considered southward runoff], then by 0.3 to track only the solids fraction, and then by 1 500 (km) average transport distance to deposition. This yields a magnitude of 6.4.

Thus, if the flood that produced the drumlins is dated to terminal Wisconsin time; this "event", of which the Erratics Train is the most visible cataform, will have out-performed the other fluvial cataforms other than, possibly, the Caribou gravels. It would only be exceeded in my tabulation by the great Klamath translation.

Geologists from earliest days, but especially from the eighteenth century [Baron Cuvier and others] recognized that a great "flood" had spread a blanket of "drift" over Europe. Thus, it comes as no surprise that an "event" 11,000 years ago had the energy and fluid medium to broadcast erratics and other debris in a thick blanket over southern Canada, the Great Lakes region, New England, the prairies of western Canada and the American midwest.

Anyone who has pondered the well-established sudden disappearance from this region of whole species of the larger ungulates [elephant, camel, horse, sloth, etc.] and their predators, while the same families of creatures continued, apparently unaffected, elsewhere in the world, will find a "flood" interpretation of prehistory convenient for explaining the facts.

Negative and Other Cataforms

The cataforms for which magnitudes have been calculated and

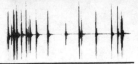
presented in these pages have all comprised excavated and displaced materials, "positive cataforms," so to speak. The sources for the moved materials are "negative" cataforms by nature. Examples of negative cataforms are the "channelled scabland" of Bretz and the crater left [if it exists] after Alvarez' impact. The negative features may be less readily quantifiable. Their intrinsic nature frustrates appraisal.

CATAFORMS OF EXOGENY
AN ASTRONOMER'S PERSPECTIVE

There is a natural intense interest among people from all walks of life in the flux of catastrophe over time. Whether it can and will affect lives is ultimately important. S.V.M. Clube, a British astronomer, has addressed this question in books and papers for over a decade. His views on cometary processes and their consequential catastrophic consequences are most recently summarized in a short paper, "The Dynamics of Armageddon".

Clube summarizes the outlook for humanity as follows:

Apollo "Earth-orbit crossing" asteroids were only recognized in the 1970s. They are now known to comprise a flux of 1,000 or more devolatilized comet fragments. This debris originated from the breakup of giant comets that were greater than 100 km in diameter.

That such comets break up readily upon being subjected to the gravitational effects of other astral bodies is emphasized by Clube, with his description of their cohesiveness as the "strength of steam-percolated coffee grains."

The Apollo asteroids cross Earth's orbit with a "frequency determined by remote tidal effects of the Galaxy on the largely unseen Oort cometary cloud...[This] mostly invisible debris [which is] remotely controlled by forces that are themselves largely unseen ... [includes Apollo asteroids] with swarms of meteoroids and dust [to] produce sequences of encounters with Earth, which survive for a few centuries, seriously disturbing climate. The timescale of the largest effects, lasting millenia [ice-ages] is that of the arrival of the giant comets themselves [i.e., 10^5-10^6 years] with similar setbacks for mankind."

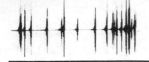

Clube goes on to develop the rationale for longer period cataclysms of $10-10$ year scales based on Galactic passages. He shows in his diagrams a fact that geologists have long puzzled over: that some of the greatest cataclysms in geological history are only recognized in one part of the Earth. My allusion to the flood event that terminated Wisconsin glaciation in North America 11,000 years ago is one of this genre. Extinctions of some large ungulates (camel, horse, etc.) were peculiar to North America at this time.

Clube does not venture into geology; but his lucid explication of the causes of cataclysm raise the point in connection with the turbulent occurrences of late Jurassic time, the "Nevadan revolution" in the Klamath Mountains and around the Pacific rim. Late Jurassic upheaval was a mainly circum-Pacific feature rather than worldwide. That fact alone commends our attention to the Clube concept of cometary origins for the geological "revolutions".

If we are now to venture to summarize permissible correlations among the ten disparate cataform features that I have quantified with magnitudes the reader needs to bear in mind that:

1. All of these fall within the last four percent of geological time. It is the features developed in this timespan that are best preserved.

2. Enormous cataclysms are recognized to have occurred in the next earlier 11% of geological time. Notable especially are the preCambrian transition, the mid-Ordovician (Caledonian), the mid-Devonian (Frasnian), and the Permian/Triassic transitions.

3. During the remaining 85% of the geological record, overprinting of cataform on cataform effectively has obscured the facts to where we may never unscramble them.

For perspective, let us represent the time remaining up to the present from the beginning of each geological time division as a percentage of total geological time. We get the following:

GEOLOGICAL TIME, PERCENTAGES

[from beginning of each time period to present]

Holocene	.003%	Triassic	6.6%
Pleistocene	.05	Permian	7.6
Pliocene	.14	Carboniferous	9.5
Miocene	.6	Devonian	10.8
Oligocene	.9	Silurian	11.6
	"E/O"	Ordovician	13.4
Eocene	1.4	Cambrian	15
Paleocene	1.7		"pC/C"
Cretaceous	3.7	Proterozoic	40
	"K/T"	Archeozoic	100
Jurassic	5.3		
	"J/K"		

The shadows cast by the processes of erosion, endogeny and the cometary wrecking balls that have disrupted Earth throughout its history obscure our vision severely on the first 85% of Earth history, preCambrian times. Detailed event sequences in the Proterozoic and Archeozoic Eras remain hidden behind the "shades of time", as Shakespeare put it. I will leave the enigmas of those times to brief treatment in Part IV of this book.

The next 11% of geological time after that first 85%, the Cambrian through middle Jurassic Periods, are still obscure enough that we are presented with conflicting data that lead to controversy. The disputed origins of the Klamath Mountain system illustrates this.

Our best hope for gaining perspective on what has been going on in evolution of our planet is inquiry into the cataforms of the last four percent of geological time. Looking into that time period has brought us to this point.

GLOBAL CATAFORMS
PERMISSIBLE CORRELATIONS

We have now examined a spectrum of cataforms. In order of decreasing age they are:

J/K	Major Klamath diapirism Possible Klamath explosivity
Cretaceous	Klamath, Sierran, and upper Columbia/Fraser mature upland "etchplain" development Klamath valley cutting, later deposition in same valleys Columbia/Fraser beach boulder or bar winnowing
K/T	Klamath explosivity and lahar release
Paleocene	Quiescence in all areas
Eocene	Saskatchewan Gravels, eastward-moving flood and boulder broadcast Columbia/Fraser valley incision
E/O	Rocky Mountain welt dilation, overthrust shedding, partial subsidence with keystone blocks dropping into present positions Rise of Wasatch Range, drainage reversal from eastward to westward Klamath possible additional explosivity and lahar releases North American tektites, microtektites, glass spherules splashed, possibly by Earth-grazing missive creating the Greenland crater-form depression and westward-moving wave resulting in Caribou plateau boulder broadcast
26,000 yr.	Lake Calgary flood, a jökulhlaup, Glenmore stratum deposited Lake Bonneville decantation
11,000 yr.	Lake Missoula jökulhlaups channelled scablands Alberta Erratics ice-rafted

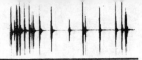

> Drumlinfields flood, drift broadcast over much of
> North America
> Lakes Bonneville and Lahonton cut off from northern
> sources by terrain dilation
> Cordilleran terrain [Canadian Rockies, Missoula,
> Bonneville] generally raised after the flood
> events

Some noteworthy aspects on each of these follow:

Late Jurassic, the "J/K" transition *(Mag. 6.9)* and the ensuing Cretaceous.

The Klamath translation cataform is part of a belt of ultramafics, volcanics, and melanged sedimentary terranes that stretch through the California motherlode series northwestward encompassing the Klamath Mountains, and thence north in a broad expanse that includes the eastern Oregon terrane of Hell's Canyon on Snake River as well as mountainous northwestern Washington, interior British Columbia and southern Alaska.

These Jurassic terranes are all elements of Carey's "megashear" between continent and Pacific basin, a wide belt of late Jurassic turmoil. Concomitant horizontal translations, dilation/relaxation spasms and dextral offsets, collectively comprised "the Nevadan orogeny," an episode of extreme environmental violence along the western margin of North America.

Major endogeny is implied by global crust additions at this time. Whether this might have been triggered by an impact from space is moot. On the scale of cataformity developed in this book the J/K episode had one hundred times the potency of the subsequent K/T "event", a perspective of sobering dimension.

The Klamaths and some other Cordilleran mountain uplifts are considered to be dated approximately to the Jurassic/Cretaceous (J/K) transition by the fossil content of conglomerates and other clastic rocks deposited on their flanks. One such fringe deposit is the Hornbrook formation near Yreka on the east flank of the Klamaths and on the southeast near the village of Ono. These deposits are still in place, 80-130 million years after emplacement on the flanks of the 135-million-year-old mountain terrane.

Contemporaneously with the early Cretaceous conglomerates

and ongoing after their deposition, the emergent highlands weathered chemically and developed red tropical soils known as laterites. A great valley system was incised as the mountains rose leaving the laterites perched high on plateaus between valleys in which marine shales and the aforesaid conglomerates were laid.

The less-deeply incised Yuba system and the mature interfluvial terrain of the Sierra Nevada, as now found preserved between the intervening and later-sculptured major canyons, was also developed in these Cretaceous times.

In the Canadian Rockies a fringing conglomerate [the Cadomin formation] was developed on the east flank of Cretaceous shoaling soon after the Jurassic-Cretaceous (J/K) transition.

These examples of flanking deposits on J/K tectogenes are a surprise if considered in terms of Lyell's "unending change" because they are preserved in situ over such long periods without change. They are somewhat indurated but not metamorphosed. Their preservation in this condition shows without doubt that the violence characteristic of the Jurassic period abated in Cretaceous time. Lyell would have expected that turmoil to have continued unabated. It did not; and for 70 million years of Cretaceous time relative peace reigned in the Klamaths. The quiescence was disrupted 200,000 years or so before the end of the Period by the misnamed "K/T event", which opened with explosive volcanism that continued for several hundred thousand years.

Above the future Rocky Mountains shoaling had developed with winnowed and reworked gravels derived from Cambrian conglomerates. As the gravel shoal emerged, the strandline retreated west.

The Pacific Ocean lapped on the west flank of the bar and the mid-continent sea on the east. Primarily being quartzite clasts, the preCambrian gravels are distinctive and visible today, reworked yet again into younger formations.

The Cretaceous-Tertiary ("K/T") transition Mag. 4.8 and Paleocene:

Quiescent Cretaceous time closed with the "K/T" period of renewed violence. Individual cataforms that I have taken up, and which may have been born of the K/T tramsition, include (1) a tsunami in Texas, (2) worldwide explosive aerosol with siderophile minerals, (3) a volcanic surge cloud in the Cordillera, and (4) Lahars flowing from proto-Mt. Shasta.

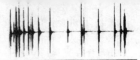
K/T features that have not been taken up, although widely recognized as part of this transition period, include (5) flood basalts (the enormous Deccan volcanic floods of India) and (6) faunal extinctions (plankton, dinosaurs). The last has been significantly overplayed as a specifically K/T phenomenon in that the extinctions were attenuated over 400,000 years.

It is hard to escape the conclusion that cometary impact is involved in these disparate occurrences: duration of the K/T "event" through several hundred thousand years; the sleeping planet bursting to life after 70 million years of slumber; resumption of destructive violence after quiescence; all this bespeaks exogeny. However, a comet swarm would seem to fill the bill much better than a single missive.

The volcanic manifestations of the period imply certainly that endogeny also was involved. Quite possibly this resulted from primary exogeny. The evidence is ambiguous but biased toward a combination of exogeny and endogeny. It should not go without notice that the 400,000-year span of the K/T period is comparable in length to the span of ice ages, which occurred in the later Pleistocene.

The close of K/T activity about 65 million years ago was followed once again by quiescence, which prevailed through Paleocene and earlier Eocene time.

Eocene and the Eocene/Oligocene "E/O" transition, Mag 6.0:

Eocene violence was first marked by the Saskatchewan gravel boulder broadcast. An eastward-moving wave crossed British Columbia churning up the enormous beach or barrier bar of coarse gravel that marked the future axis of the Rocky Mountains. It swept east across the southern Alberta prairies, dissipating its energy and broadcasting its gravel load over a 400-km reach of prairieland.

Ongoing violence in the form of tidal surging caused a deep valley system to be scoured out in the area west of the continental divide. These surging Eocene tides in the estuarine valleys, which today comprise the upper Columbia and Fraser river systems, produced most of the present spectacular relief of that region.

The tidal violence was broken abruptly by a "shot heard round the world". A missive from space had splashed eight billion tonnes or, perhaps, much more melted crustal rock and projectile into the

atmosphere and back into space. Much of this encircled the Earth and rained down in congealed form as the North American strewnfield of tektites, microtektites, and glass.

This impact may have intercepted Earth on a southward tangential trajectory such that it creased the North Atlantic seafloor, creating the Greenland crater form in the process. If so, the depression under the icecap should contain a Tertiary sedimentary infill on a glass lake. And glass should impregnate the fractured basement below that.

Extensive species extinctions occurred at this time. The cause of species extinctions is hotly debated and quite moot. Darkness, acid rain, disease, radiation, excessive heat and excessive cold are variously advocated. Combinations are likely the truth because all these things can be partial consequences of primary exogeny or endogeny in the right dosages.

An enormous tsunami swept west across northern Canada overriding the Canadian Shield, assimilating boulder deposits from rivers and beaches of the stagnant land surface. Its south-westward course served to sustain its energy as it progressed over faster rotating more southerly latitudes. The resulting broadcast of metre-sized boulders came to rest as far south as the future Caribou plateau woodland terrain of northern Alberta.

The spine of the Rocky Mountains bulged paroxysmically. The height of the welt shed plates of the sedimentary cover eastward into Alberta from British Columbia and into Montana and Wyoming from Idaho, and Utah.

After these paroxysmal events, the welt relaxed. Keystone blocks dropped inward displacing glide planes of earlier over-thrusting. After the bulge subsided, Cordilleran structure was left essentially as it is found today but at lower altitude. Thus were the Rocky Mountains built - rapidly.

What Eocene activity may have occurred in the Klamaths is unclear, although it is possible some lahars flowed from the proto-Mt. Shasta vent area in this Eocene/Oligocene transition (E/O) rather than in the Cretaceous/Tertiary (K/T) boundary "event". The ambiguity arises because the reworked counterparts of the known lahars, the Hyampom and Big Bar strata and the upper Montgomery Creek formation, have at one time and another been assigned either an Oligocene or Eocene age by various paleontologists. The lahars themselves must be older than their reworked derivative deposits.

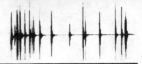

Sierra Nevada and Wasatch Mountain terrain was not sculpted mainly in the Eocene. An exception is the valley of Marsh Creek, Gilbert's "great canyon of the Bonneville River". The Wasatch valley sculpture, as in the case of the deep valleys of the Sierra Nevada, only started in the Eocene. Thirty-three million years to Pleistocene time were to pass before the necessary terrain dilation provided today's vigorous stream gradients and renewed major valley sculpture in those terrains.

Late Pleistocene, 26,000-year flood, Mag 3.0:

Cataforms created in this late Pleistocene "event" include (1) the great Calgary flood (jökulhlaup?) and (2) terrain movements, which caused massive Bonneville Lake water decantation through American Falls Lake and Lake Idaho into the Columbia River. These Bonneville and Calgary cataforms are temporally close enough together to be likely due to a single pulse of endogeny either alone or consequent upon cometary impact.

Pleistocene-Holocene transition, 11,000 years, Mag 4:

Similar coincidence in time occurs between the forty or more lake Missoula releases, the flood that accompanied the Alberta Erratics Train, and the final land movements that cut off the Bonneville and ancestral Snake Rivers from delivering water to Lakes Bonneville and Lahontan. Although far apart in space, their association in time suggests exogenic triggering of endogeny.

One might add that a "comet swarm" is attractive for accounting for the Pleistocene series of "events". From the abruptly-started and as-abruptly-terminated series of ice ages ranging over almost one-half million years, the idea of a comet swarm helps explain otherwise enigmatic suddenness.

The drumlinfields are probably correlatives with this "event", whence the magnitude of **6.4** describes it, a marked escalation.

The 200,000-year scoreboard as I rate it looks this way:

Timing, years x 1000		Magnitude	Nature of cataclysm
J/K	140,000	6.9	Endogeny rampant
K/T	65,000	4.8	Endogeny + exogeny
E/O	34,000	6.0	Exogeny certain
Pleistocene	26	3.0	Exogeny certain
Pleisto/Holocene	11	4.0 (poss. 6.4)	Exogeny certain

It is interesting that we must look so far back as the Cretaceous/Tertiary boundary to recognize major endogeny at all and as far back as the Jurassic to see irrefutable and extreme endogeny. What could have motivated great slugs of rock to move toward the surface rapidly into under-pressured chambers of the upper crust?

That this kind of diapirism actually happened twice in the Klamaths approximately 140 million years ago with such speed that the entire surface terrain was translated west and warped into arcs in the process is self-evident from the cataforms that are left behind. The great outer arc of the Klamaths must have been first. The inner arc around the Trinity ultramafic complex appears to be a superimposition and, hence, to have followed it.

Local extrusion on the erosion surface of earlier-emplaced diapirs, as described for the Trinity Complex, the Lower Coon Mountain peridotite, and the Little Red Mountain ultramafic body, are interpreted as a last stage of diapirism. Their emplacement may be due to differential bouyancy during Tertiary terrain dilation, a process that would have been facilitated by serpentinization and mylonization during their 1-2 km diapiric emergence upon the old Cretaceous surfaces. It should be kept in mind that these late-stage movements are orders of magnitude less energetic than the original 100-200 km late Jurassic injections from mantle depths; and they occurred more than 80 million years later, that is to say, after the 65 myBP K/T "event".

The fundamental question of what causes diapiric slugs to rise from mantle depths is still unanswered despite much petrological investigation that might well have turned up the answer before this. While the explanation is beyond the purview of field geology, it must accommodate field observations of:

1. Earth's evident capability for new diapir development from mantle rock with frequency that has increased over geological time.
2. The presence of hydrocarbons at deep Earth levels in crystalline as well as sedimentary terranes of the crust.
3. The constraint that volatiles could not have been retained by an accreting early Earth (further discussed in Part IV),

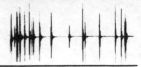

4.   The arcane processes of metals migration, flash volatility, and chaotic behavior of intrusions, [kimberlites, lamprophyres and hexagon-shaped plugs].

CARBIDE-HYDRIDE THEORY OF INNER EARTH

A regenerative process that allows gaseous emanations from deep levels of the Mantle or Core is implied by hydrocarbons [perspective #2 above] in crystalline terranes. Mineral carbides of the major rock-forming metals, silicon, iron, and nickel, among others, are regular constituents of meteorites. In that provenance they are often associated with graphite (Alexander et al, 1990). It is likely that carbides are present in the lower Mantle in pressure/ density regimes approaching those of the outer Core, 1.3 million atmospheres and 10.7 g/cm³. Exotic mineral phases should be anticipated under such conditions. **Dense metal carbides in the lower Mantle could provide a deep Earth source of carbon for hydrocarbons from those levels.**

Hydrogen, the second component, if occurring in association with the carbon, could explain observed geodynamic behavior. But because hydrogen is so light and volatile, its existence in a high pressure/temperature regime would seem problematical. This prejudgment arises because we think of hydrogen as the gas and ions of our surface environment.

Metal sponges of iron and other metals are known as a means of storing hydrogen fuel in the form of metal-hydrogen compounds known as hydrides. Multiples of molecular equivalent weights of hydrogen can be sequestered in this way. That is to say, many atoms of hydrogen are stored by each atom of the storing metal. Under surface conditions the hydrides dissociate if pressure is reduced, and gas can be drawn off.

The density of Earth's outer Core is about 26% greater than that of metallic iron. If only a small part of this is attributable to hydrides the available hydrogen content could be staggering. I suggest that Earth has a metal hydride component in its Core, as Gottfried has theorized (1990).

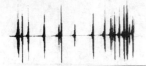

The origin of hydrides in Earth's Core poses a problem, however. The most widely-held view of the process by which Earth originated is that it accreted by gravitational accumulation of primordial debris. This mode of development would have been inhospitable to preservation of gaseous hydrogen or hydrides, which are vulnerable to pressure release. Gottfried's theory, on the other hand, provides a rationale whereby a primordial Earth rich in hydrides could have originated within our Solar System.

An alternative might be the capture by the Solar System of a hydride-rich proto-planet. Earth accretion could have proceeded by accumulation around such a captured body while preserving its hydride-rich Core.

In any case, hydrogen and hydrocarbons do rise from depth in many places; and I suggest that the existence of hydrides and carbides is the best explanation of why this should be so. I postulate that dense phases of carbides occur in metastable equilibrium at core level until somehow perturbed, perhaps by the shock waves of an impact.

Perturbation destabilization then allows SiC to dissociate and its carbon and silicon to link up with available free hydrogen from the hydrides as hydrocarbons and their silicon analogues, the silanes. A bubble of hydrocarbon and silane volatiles so generated would have the convective mobility to gassify, lubricate, brecciate and expel diapirs of whatever solid material stood in its way to the surface. A pulsating ascent, as proposed by Gold on timescales that could be minutes, days, or years, would yield the diapiric array that geology reveals. The mystery of deep Earth volatiles and many other phenomena become understandable in this manner.

The diameters of Core and lower Mantle, now the hosts to metal hydrides and carbides could have been larger than at present. Exhalation from the Core and lower Mantle of hydrocarbons, silanes and entrained solids would have resulted in contraction of Core and lower Mantle along with expansion of upper Mantle and Crust. It is not unreasonable that the proto-Earth could have had a thin, perhaps continuous crust over its entire surface as first proposed by Richard Owen in 1857 (Thompson, 1988). This later became known as "Pangean" crust, a concept that is supported by most plate tectonics and expanding Earth theorists.

Mass for mass, a primordial all-core Earth with a density of 10.7 g/cm³ and core diameter of 10 240 km could have evolved to its present core diameter of 6 972 km, a 68% reduction, by wastage through the exhalation of volatiles. Concomitant additions to Mantle and Crust would have increased Earth's diameter by 25% to its present size. This scenario of core attrition and external expansion can account for the present outer Earth layering.

Gottfried proposes a 30 g/cm³ original core, thus allowing for early-Earth expansion on a much greater scale and leading up to the formation of the Pangean Crust. Present carbide-hydride reactions, I suggest, continue, still violent but much less so than in times when Pangean Crust was being created.

Volatile silanes rising with hydrocarbons have a special role in this system. They transfer silicon from inner to outer Earth levels. Silicon, mobilized into silane form, reacts with water upon first coming into contact with it. This is mainly at the lower crustal levels. Silica and silicates are deposited and hydrogen is released. Silicon from this source is proposed as the basis for the creation of the Pangean Crust and for continent incrementation through geological time. It is, as well, the agency for conduit plugging and, thus, an initiator of mantle chamber explosion conditions.

Hydrogen released from the silanes along with already-ambient hydrocarbons forces the silica and silicate seals [as at Gros Brukkaros] and reopens the vents, explosively or otherwise.

In addition to explaining diapirism itself, the injection of deep Earth exhalatives into the Crust can explain mid-crustal melting as an effect of heat released by the silane reaction with water as well as release of heat of crystallization of diapiric ultramafic magmas. Such heat, by melting the host rock, is capable of initiating granitization, migmatization, and volcanism.

The spasmodic release of these rising volatiles, in their violent surges from chamber to chamber in the plastic lower crust results in the energy releases of deep earthquakes, an enigma up to now because of the presumable incapacity for plastic crust to behave in the fashion of stress buildup and release ascribed to the earthquake mechanism [incorrectly] by the popular doctrine.

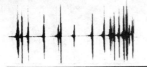

In summary, I am advancing the carbide-hydride hypothesis of inner Earth as a general theory of endogeny, an explanation to all the following:

1. Diapir initiation.
2. Continent formation and Mantle chamber explosions.
3. Hydrocarbons, carbon and hydrogen from deep Earth sources.
4. Dilation and collapse of crustal welts and the development of melanges and mylonites.
5. Mid-crustal melting, granitization, magmatism, and mobilization and volcanic ejection of crustal materials.
6. Earthquake energy, its source and mode of application.
7. The origin of quartz segregations, high-silica quartzites and rhyolitic volcanics.

PERSPECTIVE FOR THE FUTURE

S.V.M. Clube made the proposal that Earth's predicament arose when a giant comet of greater than 100-km diameter was involved in a major fragmentation in about 3,000 B.C. He said that debris from the fragmentation is threatening Earth. Among the manifestations of the disintegrated behemoth are meteor showers, some Apollo asteroids, boulder impactors, and larger objects.

Clube lists implied cometary involvement in historic destructive events. For example, the time of the fall of Rome followed "a significant fragmentation in the Taurid stream in the 4th century, A.D." At 441 A.D. Clube interprets an historic major catastrophe to have occurred in Britain, Spain and China. A "strange comet" was followed by a "darkened sky". The "event" was reported as the "ruin of Britain, [when] fire fell from heaven and did not die down until it had burned the whole surface of the island." The description is strangely reminiscent of scenes reported in Chicago area newspapers on the Chicago fire ("Mrs. O'Leary's comet").

It is noteworthy that the 3,000-year comet breakup launched comets that were devastating to civilization but minuscule by comparison with at least two events of the last 26,000 years, either of which would have entirely wiped out civilization in the regions of their occurrence.

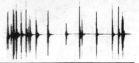

Clube points out the 350-km body, Chiron, far out in the Solar System. In 50,000 to 100,000 years the astronomers anticipate this body will be deflected into an Earth-crossing orbit. The monster is 42 times the size of the projectile that is proposed by Alvarez to have produced worldwide destruction and, by my calculation, magnitude 6.0 geological cataforms. If this is the outlook as seen in today's skies and from the history of the last 3,000 years, one could hardly disagree that our future is bleak indeed.

The two Pleistocene events I have discussed, those of 26,000 and 11,000 years ago, are likely no more than typical of many repetitive events of the Pleistocene, for which the surficial geological evidence has been destroyed by erosion.

Preserved features of cataform nature that I have recognized and discussed are the few I know something about from personal experience. They are no more than a sampling of preserved cataforms of the world. Many more will be found by anyone curious enough to seek them out.

In the Mediterranean region, for example, the literature records overturned slabs of mountain size in the Apennines (Hsu, 1967). And occupying most of the Peloponnesian Peninsula, a great debris avalanche of chaotic blocks of rock foreign to the host terrain, an "allochthon" in geological terms, has slid 160 km or more from the northeast on a nearly flat glide surface (Temple, 1968). All parts of the world have hyper-energy features; and much can be done to describe and record them properly as the products of cataclysm. The geological profession of this century has only begun to recognize the pervasive importance of cataclysm in shaping modern scenery.

The belatedness with which this recognition has come is partly attributable to the fact that civilization has had 300 years of fortuitous environmental calm. In this interlude population has doubled several times, science has blossomed, and new social organizations have proliferated.

Another retardant to recognition of the significance of cataclysm in the shaping of our world has been the religious idea that man's presence on Earth serves higher purposes, and that mankind must, therefore, be protected from extinction by a benign

creator. This idea has been incorporated into the twentieth century religion known as humanism as the widespread notion that the individual has inherent rights [life, liberty, pursuit of happiness, a clean and hospitable environment, etc.] and that the environment is basically and normally benign.

These misperceptions have been fostered by fortuitous environmental peace disregardful of the contrary implications from mythology and historic records of "events" of our times as set forth by Clube. The outlook is not encouraging for an environment of enduring peace. For mankind to have faith that "mother" nature will adhere to gradualism is no better than self-administered anesthesis against the prognosis for exogeny in the intermediate term, 50,000-100,000 years. As Clube puts it, "nature has Armageddon in store".

The reader's thoughts may well be redirected to the destruction of the primordial forests that lined the shores of Pleistocene Lake Lahontan. The magnificence of the now-ghostly giants was smothered in cinders, their verdure overwhelmed by ash leaving only sagebrush and desolation. Armageddon for the cedar forest came with cutoff of the flow of northern waters, a first stage of endogeny. The suffocating ashfall was a second stage, and for the forest, the coup de grâce.

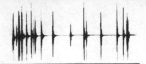

PART IV

OXYGEN, WATER, VIRUSES AND ICE AGES

FOUR ENIGMAS

Dynamic cataforms of Parts I and II have been quantified in Part III insofar as possible. There are still other manifestations of environmental hyper-energy events where the relics of cataclysm are enigmatic. Part IV will consider the oxygen content of air, the origins of Earth's water, the starting and ending of ice ages and the inplications for a relationship between them and the life systems of our planet.

Water and oxygen, unique in the Solar System and essential for the biota, both have been proposed as products of hyper-energy "events". What sources can be accredited with these unique planetary envelopes? The oxygen is known to be renewed by photosynthesis. Cometary water enters the upper atmosphere as an ongoing process of unknown magnitude.

The biota itself alters physical environment by regeneration of oxygen from carbon dioxide, a process that has been taken farther in the "Gaia" theory, which holds that living matter has inborn capability of altering its environment to fit its needs. This latter idea will not be resolved by geology, but should be borne in mind in any appraisal of the scheme of things.

ORIGINS OF EARTH'S WATER

William Whiston, Newton's successor in the Royal Society, advocated the idea in 1691 that Earth's water originated from comets. Whiston is said to have been purged from his eminent post for that audacious "nonsense".

Ocean waters have a volume estimated at 1.37 billion km^3 (330 million mi^3), 1.4 x 10^{18} tonnes. A further 2.2-2.6 x 10^{18} tonnes is estimated to be locked into mineral structure in crustal rocks,

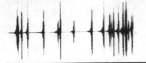

1.5-1.85 "ocean equivalents", one could say. Mantle mass is 169 times crust mass and core mass is 79 times crust mass. How many equivalent oceans are locked into those realms no one knows.

Majority opinion among geologists is that surficial water has been "exhaled" from the interior over long geological time, a process known as "outgassing". Mean surface elevation of the planet is already 2 430 m (7,972 feet) below sea level. If outgassing is the source of this water, the amount still available from the interior of Earth is enormous, and continued exhalation will be unmitigable disaster for mankind and other non-aquatic biota!

But, perhaps outgassing is not the source of most of the water. Hoyle addressed the question (1986), quoting Harrison Brown on a central question, the survivability of free water vapor in the hot climate of an accreting planet:

"In view of the large fractionation factors, it would appear that during the process of Earth formation the mechanism was such as to prohibit the retention of an appreciable fraction of any substance that existed at that time primarily in the gaseous state."

The case for water locked in minerals would differ, however, being specific to each mineral and to each level of pressure/ temperature conditions. Thus, we are left without a definite answer to the problem. There is no escaping the fact that indigenous water could not have survived early Earth formation processes as vapor or liquid. The interior of Earth, probably holding many "ocean equivalents" of water locked into mineral forms, may have outgassed a large or only a small portion of its present ocean, while the other fraction would be from cometary sources.

Giving strength to the argument against an outgassing source is the contrasting situation on the sister planet, Venus. If the two planets are, indeed, of similar origins, one would expect them to have comparable hydrospheres. In fact, Earth has a great excess of hydrogen over Venus. This occurs as water, methane, and hydrous mineral combinations in the Crust and, perhaps in the mantle. Hydrogen likely occurs as hydrides in the Core.

Taken in context with Harrison Brown's constraint on preser-

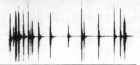

vation of volatiles during accretion, the origin of the vastly different regimes of water on the two planets cannot be resolved with finality. It may either be attributed to Earth having core hydrides that are absent in Venus; or it may be the result of a chance encounter by Earth with a water/methane-rich comet, a fortuitous event not shared by Venus.

COMETARY ORIGIN OF GLACIAL ICE

INITIATION OF GLACIATION by infalling cometary volatiles is a radical incrementation of the cometary water source idea. I find the idea appealing because it is supported, "by a few facts" as Darwin would have said. Here are some of them:

Rapid refrigeration of large animal carcasses. The semi-preserved state of some large animal bodies in Pleistocene ice of the Siberian and Alaskan arctic has been recognized in the popular press for the last century. While the carcasses have been found hardly table ready, they are said to have been consumed by hungry dogs. To achieve even this preservation without putrefaction required refrigeration of the huge bodies at rates more rapid than those employed in modern commercial freezing. Donald W. Patten (1978) first suggested the icefall idea.

Patten sought to establish that the icefall had to be fast. There are many facts supportive of this. The one I like best is a photograph of a baby mammoth *standing encased in ice.* His burial was necessarily fast. Ice must have packed in so quickly around his body that *it supported him before he suffocated and fell over. That required an icefall such that the beast was encased in partially-compacted firn-like ice within just a few minutes!* It baffles me that anyone would try to explain such an event by gradualist processes.

Patten went on to make a third point, that **global distribution of glacial ice does not conform to the coldest regions.** It avoided altogether some large parts of northern Siberia, Alaska and northwestern Canada. The maximum ice thickness in North America was found in subarctic latitudes.

To explain this, Patten proposed that the icefall could have been made up of particles carrying electrical charges. These, he theorized, were deflected by the magnetic field of Earth and

channelled through the torus of the Van Allen belts, which encircle the magnetic poles. Whether or not ice particles could carry such a charge, it seems unlikely that there would be sufficient magnetic attraction or repulsion for infalling ice crystals to be redirected. Nevertheless, Patten hits on an important engima, the unexpected topology of continental ice growth. **Ice buildup was evidently not controlled by climate.**

Thus, we have three "facts" concerning the Pleistocene that are not very convenient to explain, extreme cold, rapid precipitation, and non-climatic topology. To Patten's ideas I would add two more:

Continental ice sheet buildup on essentially flat ground under subarctic conditions is inadequately explained by gradualist doctrine.

Mainstream thought considers that as little as 6° C drop in mean annual temperature in the Adirondacks could trigger a new "ice age". I can accept this for the case of mountain glacier growth in the Adirondacks or anywhere that wind shadows created by the terrain would protect ice as it built up to a mass sufficient in size for an atmospheric cyclonic downdraft to be established. Such an air flow gives weather protection to the Greenland ice cap.

Absent terrain protection, the thermal inversion necessary for a cyclone to develop and to be preserved year-round, could not occur above a seasonal snowfield. Glacier growth under these conditions would not be robust.

This is the situation as I see it on the relative flatland of the Canadian or Fennoscandian shields. Any temporary high-pressure systems that might develop over a growing ice mass would be swept away each summer.

It is likely impossible for a glacial mass to have grown in subarctic Canada without pre-existing permanent cyclonic protection.

The hospitality of the Antarctic shield to glacier growth is inherently much greater than that of the shields of the northern hemisphere because Antarctica has significantly more elevation,

more terrain relief, less insolation, and, most important, less warm airflow across its great isolated expanse.

Sea-level changes are another aspect of geology that are said to demonstrate the fluctuation between ice wastage and new buildup ("interstadials"). Forty or more of these fluctuations are believed to have occurred and should be reflected in low and high sea levels respectively. Today we are thought to be living in an interstadial, the sea level being high. The strandlines representing the forty "ice ages" are supposedly submerged and largely inaccessible.

Whether many submerged strandlines with ice-age origin even exist is doubtful. I am impressed that few have been found, although numerous submerged wave-cut surfaces at deeper levels in the oceans are known.

The most significant "fact" in connection with Pleistocene sea levels would seem to be that a worldwide rise of about 100 m from the glacial low stand occurs. Darwin called attention to this long ago. But what levels the sea occupied before that general low stand is less clear. The opportunity for dispute arises from the fact that coastlines often give evidence of having been highly mobile even in recent times.

As examples, in California perched wave-cut benches and the recently drained Great Valley tell of general emergence. Farther north fjord shorelines of western Canada and Alaska attest to net submergence. In the vicinity of the Hudson Canyon off New York, apparent rise of sea level through Pleistocene time has been approximately double the amount attributable to ice sheet melting, 200 m instead of 100 m. There, we must conclude, *net submergence* has occurred, unrelated presumably, to continental ice.

Thus, the evidence is weak for forty or more neatly arranged rises and falls of sea level. Instead, an over-arching one-hundred-metre rise in sea level appears to be supported. This can be better ascribed to cometary ice accretion during Pleistocene time than to any other cause.

Cometary injecta to the atmosphere is a general subject that has been dealt with extensively over some years by Hoyle and Wickramasinghe (1978, 1981, 1983). They establish to my satisfaction that ablated comet material includes organic compounds,

primitive microscopic life forms, and rock and metal dusts, and that these all reach Earth in a continuing shower.

Most recently Frank and Yeates (1988) have focussed directly on impacting icy comets. Frank predicted on purely theoretical grounds in 1986 that some ten million tiny comets (100 tons average) per year (one each three seconds) in sizes of 8-16 feet in diameter intersect the upper atmosphere. Yeates was able to take photographs that seem to confirm this. Their numbers are such that the ocean would gain significant water from them.

In conflict with the Frank and Yeates claim is the fact that the moon should be receiving similar micro-impactors, an occurrence that has not been recognized. Then, if the theory is true, Venus also, should be gaining water, perhaps making up for what it missed in the earlier rounds.

Frank's theory, which is receiving much current attention, is important and interesting. The true numbers of icy comets impacting Earth's atmosphere may be less than he has proposed, but still significant.

In conclusion then, the fragmentary evidence we have to work with supports the following outlook:

(1) Cometary arrival accounts for most water of the Earth's hydrosphere after early Earth cooled. Repeated comet swarms best fit the facts.

(2) Outgassing has been a significant but lesser contribution to the hydrosphere. Despite large water volumes held in mineral combinations, this source for the oceans has been a lesser contributor to surface waters in my judgment.

(3) Sudden onset of glaciation may have been associated with massive infall of ice in the form of hail or frost.

Frost from space originating as ablation debris from comet tails, as proposed by William Whiston, could have provided the water. Swarms of comets, large or small, could result from breakup of a larger comet or perturbation from the Oort cloud on periodic passages of the Solar System through it.

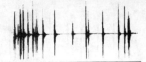

ICE AGE STARTS AND ENDINGS

The start of an ice age by a "frost fall" is an intriguing idea, albeit speculative. It is the only way I can see how a thick ice blanket could form in the first place *under normal climatic conditions.* A cyclonic down-flow of cold air from aloft protecting the ice from its temperate surroundings, should have given it a chance of attracting massive additional precipitation. The full 3 000 to 4 000 m buildup of the North American continental glacier in this way becomes a believable possibility from my point of view.

A different climatic scenario is developed by Hoyle in his study of ice-age mechanisms. He shows that water vapor in the upper atmosphere arrives through ocean evaporation and warms that portion of the atmosphere by releasing its latent heat in the process of liquefaction. This process holds the temperature from falling below -40° C. Slightly below that temperature spontaneous ice crystals form.

Hoyle's theory is that such cirrus ice crystal formation can reflect 90% of solar energy. Unreplenished, the reserves of ocean heat would within ten years be exhausted. The ability of the ocean thereafter to provide the essential evaporation to the upper atmosphere would have been destroyed. The entrenched ice age would have become irreversible.

The most likely scenario, Hoyle thinks, whereby ice crystals would proliferate in the upper atmosphere, is meteorite impact. The aerosol thrown up would contain enough fine material to keep it aloft through the required ten years. Volcanic action, one alternative to meteorite impact, carries less energy, insufficient in all likelihood to raise sufficient aerosol for it to remain aloft for ten years. Hoyle thinks three cubic kilometres of ice crystals distributed worldwide would be sufficient to trigger an ice age in the foregoing manner.

Micrometeorite impact into the upper atmosphere, the third possible scenario, was inadequate, Hoyle felt. That was, of course, before the Frank and Yeates' observations. I would think a preferrable scenario to Hoyle's meteorite would be for the Earth to pick up super-cold ice in a passage through the ablation cloud from a large comet tail.

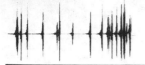

Space debris of this type, if moving at a velocity close to that of the Earth would not have to be slowed down much on impact with the upper atmosphere. At velocities of perhaps no more than five or ten m/sec the smaller particles would be slowed without much frictional heating. Coarser fragments infalling could have provided the ice, which overwhelmed, buried, and rapidly froze the large animal herds. Smaller particles could have remained aloft as cirrus haze.

This scenario avoids snags inherent in Hoyle's meteorite. Firstly, if an impact had started each of the forty ice buildups, aerosols reporting them should be showing up in the Greenland and Antarctic ice cores. These are not recognized, so far. Secondly, the chance of Earth passing through a comet ablation cloud and acquiring three km^3 of finely divided ice is much greater than the chance for a direct comet impact sufficient for the purpose. Forty such impacts are not reasonably to be expected.

Termination of "ice ages" is another process that needs to be considered as a possible hyper-energy phenomenon. My theory in 1977 of the termination of Wisconsin continental glaciation called for its disruption by inundation. A near-Earth passage of an asteroid [a term now used with equivalence to mean a spent comet] was proposed to have resulted in the Calgary Silt and Alberta Erratics Train about 11,000 years ago.

Since then, the charcoal in the Calgary Silt flood deposit has shown that formation to be 26,000 years in age. The Erratics are still considered products of the 11,000-year "event".

In the "event" of 26,000 yBP a comet most likely set the forests ablaze. Then, some 15,000 years later, at the termination of Wisconsin time, another enormous flood, this one represented by the drumlinfields and Alberta Erratics Train, provides us compelling evidence once again for comet involvement. In this "event" the comet impact into glacial ice produced such a quantity of water that it evidently submerged much of Canada and the northeastern and northern midwestern United States to depths of one to two km.

Recent ice core analyses from Greenland imply a sudden end to the last "ice age". W. Dansgaard of the Danish Geological Survey reports (June 15, 1989, Nature) that "7°C warming

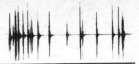

occurred within 20 years at the end of the 'Younger Dryas' [the European term for Wisconsin time equivalent], 10,700 years BP". A comet could account for this suddenness as well as for the aforesaid flooding.

The negative information on this point is that ice core data has yet to provide evidence that any anomalously large volume of ice was deposited suddenly. Neither does it show an aerosol appropriate for a large comet strike into rock. However, the actual comet may not have been so large. Its task of melting the glacier could have been accomplished with a Tunguska-like strike by a projectile of about .3 to .5 km diameter on a trajectory tangential to Earth. Its energy would of necessity have been much larger than the projectile that excavated Meteor Crater; but it need not have approached the energy of the one-km Ries impactor.

To explain the ending of ice ages, Hoyle's theory is that a dusting of the upper atmosphere with metal dust is the best option. Metal dust, which would be mainly iron, some nickel, and lesser amounts of other metals, would absorb solar heat rapidly and raise upper atmosphere temperature above the -40°C critical level, thus causing immediate vaporization of the ice crystal haze.

To get metal dust into the stratosphere would require an iron meteorite impactor. Since an impact "event" of this nature would leave its fallout signature in Greenland and Antarctic ice, the theory fails because such a signature does not appear to exist.

A better scenario, I believe, is my .3 - .5 km Tunguska-like body. Hoyle suggests that the Tunguska meteor may have been travelling at the unusual speed of 70 000 km/sec, the approximate upper limit for the Apollo asteroids. With that enormous energy a large Tunguska-like body would have sent aloft enough water vapor to melt the ice crystal haze instantly. This scenario for the 11,000-year termination of the Wisconsin/Upper Dryas ice age is a best fit for all the data.

THE OXYGEN CATASTROPHE

Life on Earth is perceived as the perpetual victim of catastrophe, never its active cause. An attempt to view man as enemy

of man's environment and, hence, of man himself, has only recently become popular through the environment movement. Let us examine what some biologists think occurred in an earlier Earth aeon.

More than two billion years ago, the Archean seas teemed with bacterial life, which flourished largely on hydrogen, methane, and sulphur. The hot, humid, perpetually-cloudy atmosphere was deficient in oxygen a toxin to most members of the Archean biota. Life forms that could tolerate oxygen and thrive while releasing oxygen from hydrogen and sulphur compounds were mainly still in the future. Nevertheless, the blue-green algae did exist; and *some life forms were transferring oxygen to ferrous iron as a part of their metabolic processes.* This is known from the earliest rock records, 3.8 billion years in age.

Biologists Margulis and Sagan in their fascinating book, "Micro Cosmos", describe the conversion of Earth's atmosphere from hydrogen-rich to oxygen-rich as an "oxygen holocaust", the "greatest pollution crisis Earth has ever known". The "event" is believed to have ensued after some obscure evolutionary step by the cyanobacteria (blue-green algae), which quite suddenly developed a capability of extracting their hydrogen requirements from water by its dissociation through the process of photosynthesis.

The "event" of transforming the atmosphere from reducing to oxidizing that marked this development is thought to have been a rapid one, a perception that may be exaggerated by its antiquity. After two billion years, the evidence is murky, if not inscrutable. That far in the past one can overlook a few million years.

When oxygen was released to the environment by the cyanobacteria, one profound immediate result was precipitation of great quantities of di-valent ferrous iron as tri-valent ferric oxides. Another profound change was that the chemical weathering of rocks began.

For existing Archean life forms, Margulis and Sagan aver that the event was a death sentence, a holocaust, as they express it. How fast this change may have come about is difficult to demonstrate. In any case, when it happened, the atmospheric concentration of free oxygen increased by a factor of 210,000 times.

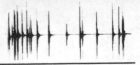

Bacterial growth under favorable conditions is very fast. Margulis and Sagan give a theoretical growth potential from a single cell to 2^{288} cells as four days! That number is larger than the entire number of protons in the Universe. Others say this multiplication process would take a few weeks. In any case, we can all agree the process could be fast.

Sir Fred Hoyle and his associate, Chandra Wickramasinghe show in their books, "Diseases from Space" and others, that viruses are theoretically capable of surviving entry into Earth's atmosphere from space. They theorize that virus-sized organisms, genes, germs, viruses, etc., are incubated in comet interiors and ablated from the comets by the solar wind as the comets reach perihelion. Once in interplanetary space, the organic microdebris orbits the sun awaiting perturbation and interception by passing planetary bodies. The truly astonishing ability of bacteria to adapt to hostile environments, including those of high radiation, is presented to establish that these micro-organisms could have survived in space until intercepted by Earth.

The Hoyle-Wickramasinghe theory asserts that virus arrivals have caused most of history's great epidemics of the viral type. The Black Death of the middle ages and the 1918 influenza epidemic fall into this category. Each of these epidemics spread erratically, by-passing islands of seeming immunity and striking new communities faster than man could travel in those days. The evidence presented shows conclusively that major leaps in the spread of these diseases cannot be attributed to contagion and reasonably can be due to viral invasion of the planet.

Subsequently, Hoyle and Wickramasinghe developed the idea that genes, which control specific organs or characteristics in diverse life forms (the gene responsible for an eye, for example), could have arrived from space in the same way as disease-causing viruses.

Sudden additions of like physical features among diverse life forms can be explained in this way. The theory neatly accounts for the heretofore puzzling fact that features of likeness occur in otherwise unrelated life forms. The eye is a striking example, occurring, as it does, commonly in forms as diverse as the octopus and mammals. Evolution of physical features that could not have

evolved incrementally becomes understandable through this idea.

If one can accept that Earth has been subject to repetitive "salting" by genes from space, one then can understand that such genes are the explanation for speciation. In evolutionary chains Hoyle and Wickramasinghe's theory asserts that **there never were any "missing links"**. No wonder none has ever been found!

Instead of gradual evolution of features [such as the eye], which could not have evolved incrementally, genes from space have made the changes sudden. They have done this by entering cells, re-programming their DNA, and giving them new features over-night. Entirely new species appear in this manner, in parallel in different life forms, all at the same time, and with the speed of an epidemic.

Fully blown and functional characteristics, sometimes redundant and only partially used can thusly be acquired. A case in point could be the brain of man. No impulse exists that would promote Darwinian evolution of the under-utilized and unnecessary capabilities of this remarkable organ.

Let us now return to the "oxygen holocaust", which might have been caused by arrival of unheralded genes from space as the Earth passed through a suitably "polluted" comet tail. One can imagine oxygen-tolerant microbes raining upon an Archean, hot, methane-rich, watery atmosphere in which primitive ("prokaryote") bacteria pervade every droplet of mist. The newly-arrived viruses from space use oxygen themselves; and they are immediately welcomed by the prokaryotes because they provide life-sustaining hydrogen to their hosts.

The visitor genes stay on, one at least, often a great number more, in every host cell, becoming known as "mitochondria". The resulting symbiotic cells make possible the new life forms, the "eukaryotes". All life above the level of bacteria falls in this classification. Intercession by mitochondria saves host cells from oxygen poisoning; and it provides the cells with essential hydrogen. The virus from space has thus, symbiotically, become essential to most life on Earth.

Interesting, and indicative of the origins of mitochondria as separate organisms, is their ability to reproduce themselves independently of the host cell's own reproduction system.

The conversion process may or may not have amounted to the gaseous shell of the planet becoming a giant reaction chamber. But that question is merely one of rate. Whether the process took much time or not in our conception of time, it happened rapidly in geological terms. Foreign photosynthetic bacteria, once dispersed in a nutrient-rich, oxygen-poor gas medium, could have extracted the hydrogen of its water vapor and released oxygen in quantities sufficient to provide the 21% component of today's atmosphere.

Unfortunately, geological and biological facts do not support the "holocaust" theory. The blue-green algae were on Earth precipitating some ferric iron long before they became the dominant life forms. The elegant concept of an "oxygen holocaust" did not occur as Margulis and Sagan contend.

Iron Formations of the World

Photosynthetic release of oxygen is one way oxygen could have been generated on Earth. The biological transfer of oxygen without its release as a gas is another. Working on water or methane, bacteria such as *Pedomicrobium* (Hoyle, 1983) or *Eosphaerra tyleri* (Laberge, 1989) were oxidizing ferrous iron in the Archean ocean long before the atmosphere became oxygenated, some as early as 3.8 Ga (billion years ago).

The main deposits of iron formation, however, awaited the oxygenation of the atmosphere. These iron formations are distinctive deposits of the period 2.5 to 1.9 Ga. They developed in great profusion in the one period, a six-hundred-million year span. A few smaller deposits occur in younger sedimentary suites.

One suggestion as to the origin of the iron formations was made by Hoyle, as mentioned above. The bacterium *Pedomicrobium* is present on Earth and in meteorites in abundance. Often its associations in meteorites include an encrustation of precipitated native metal. Thus, this bacterium appears a good candidate for deposition of the iron formation *before atmospheric oxygenation*.

Laberge, a recognized expert on iron formation, shows con-

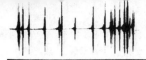

vincingly that no *single "event"* could explain the geological facts. He finds that the iron formations are *marine deposition* brought about by a microscopic, siliceous, organism called *Eosphaerra tyleri*, which had photosynthetic capability. The idea that all iron precipitation occurred in a single "event" is simply not true. Neither is it true that the iron is mainly a sub-aerial deposit. Present knowledge is too scanty to establish a clear linkage between marine deposition of ferric iron and oxygenation of the atmosphere.

These facts leave us without an explanation for the repetitive nature of the depositions over a lengthy period. We must accept that there were successive "events" of oxygenation and reduction of the atmosphere accompanied by flourishings of *E. tyleri* and, perhaps, *Pedomicrobium*.

How the atmosphere could return to reducing conditions after thorough oxygenation and iron deposition is unclear. Hoyle suggests that buried biomass could have been exposed and periodically oxidized. The numerous graphite strata in Archean rock could be the compressed and metamorphosed remains of such biomass. But there are equally numerous coal horizons in younger terrain. These, along with petroleum seepages, do not reduce the present atmosphere. Thus, it is unlikely the Archean biomass could have done so.

We must, therefore, be dealing with a process of scrubbing oxygen from the atmosphere. If such a process exists, it must be long disused. We should hope it remains disused! The initial process repeatedly provided oxygen, which the later process removed. The return to reducing environment may have occurred after the oxygenating agents had exhausted either the available ferrous iron or the active oxygen of the atmosphere. Organic processes are certainly involved. Their nature is not known.

Oxygen from Water Dissociation in the Upper Atmosphere

An alternate possibility that has been suggested for producing atmospheric oxygen is dissociation of water in the upper atmosphere. Dissociation of water vapor by ultraviolet radiation is

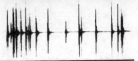

proposed as a mechanism whereby light hydrogen can diffuse into space while oxygen can accumulate in the atmosphere (T.A. Heppenheimer, Reason Magazine, Jan., 1990).

If this process can be shown to operate with quantitative sufficiency to regenerate the oxygen of Earth's atmosphere, the biotic contribution to atmospheric oxygen may be no more than one of partial maintenance. But, should this be so, the question of what produced the oxygen in the first place is reopened.

Why the dissociation process would have commenced after 1.6 billion years of Earth history only to be reversed repeatedly over the next 600 million years, is not clear. I would feel more comfortable with a dissociation process connected to the "solar wind", atomic particle flow from the sun, or with particle radiation from space, an "astral wind", so to speak. Such irradiation from space would have the much increased potential needed to perform massive dissociation of water vapor in Earth's atmosphere. This, then, is a second possible means of rapid oxygenation of the Archean reducing atmosphere. These conditions could have expedited the iron deposition by E. tyleri and Pedomicrobium.

Reducing Conditions Reestablished

No suggestion has been made as to how the reducing conditions were restored after each oxygenation "event". The possibilities are all pure speculation. One is a comet carrying reducing compounds (cyanide, hydrocarbon, hydrogen, etc.). This is not supported, however, by the atomic makeup of comet tails, which are known to carry oxygen, carbon, hydrogen, and nitrogen in about the same ratios as they occur in life forms (Hoyle, 1983).

Volcanism is another possibility. It could release similar materials into the environment. This idea fails in that high sulphur content accompanies explosive volcanism. A characteristic of iron formation is a dearth of sulphur.

The best choice could be the arrival of microbes in micro-debris that orbits the sun after ablation from comets. The microbes could have thrived for a time. Then, upon exhausting their favored

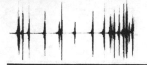

sustenance, they could have withered and gone extinct. This scenario could have been repeated for each of the iron deposition episodes.

A Summary: Oxygen, Genes, and the Environment of Violence

Hoyle and Wickramasinghe may be entirely right that man should look not to simian adaptations but to the cometary gene pool as the source of his distinguishing characteristics. Here, as in so much natural science, grandly intricate systems have arisen out of background chaos. The array of organisms of our present world as well as its multitude of extinct forms may, indeed, owe their variety to the cometary gene pool. Its tiny genetic component parts, virus-size particles able to survive entry to the atmosphere, may, indeed, have infected us with diseases or brought about the genetic changes known as evolution of species.

The science of Copernicus had succeeded in showing most educated people by Lyell's time that man and his world are not the center of the Solar System or Universe. The anthropocentricity of Ptolemy was discredited. But to this day biologists still hold to the idea that life originated on Earth. Anthropocentrism is dead; biocentrism thrives, "error surely as grave as Ptolemy's" (Hoyle, 1983).

Where Lyell held to a quest for perfection, applying reason and trying to find conformance to his preconceived hypotheses of natural order, one hundred fifty-five years later we now can see that Lyell's simple order does not exist. Instead, we are recognizing new systematics emerging from the chaos. The outlook is one of non-linearity, at the same time grand, beautiful, and challenging.

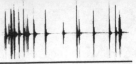

The Environmental Anagram that is geology, is a brew of Violence. Degradation by Cometary Wrecking Balls on the one hand and Endogeny on the other is balanced by growth and life. The search for the whole truth will surely be limited by man's time on Earth. Nevertheless, a search for solutions, an attempt to decode nature's Anagram awards the individual with a sense of great fulfillment as new truths emerge from the chaos. This is what I have found and what I have tried to present in these pages. Solutions are available to anyone who has the spirit, patience and careful eye for deciphering the glyphs and tracery of Cataclysm Cast in Stone.

EPILOGUE

Where do the ideas in this book originate? One forgets the diversity of sources that have entered the banks of memory and become available for resolving problems. Surprisingly, most of the basic ideas advanced in this book were current before 1840. Drawing on Susan Thompson's "Chronology of geological thinking from antiquity to 1899" (1988) one finds that:

Pythagoras, 5th century, BC, observed that **running water cuts valleys.**

Nicholas Steno, 1669, observed that the **history of Earth's development could be read in the rocks.**

William Whiston, 1691, Newton's protegé averred that the deluge **was caused (at least in part) by condensation of vapor from a comet tail.** Whiston's dalliance with comets compromised his professional status in the eyes of some colleagues, who thought he had gone daft.

Benoit Maillet, 1720, determined that **Earth is two billion years old, man 400,000.** Not bad for a seventeenth century man. Notice how obscure his name is in the scientific firmament.

Edmund Halley, 1724, deduced that **a comet struck Earth and caused mountains to be formed from sea-bottom sediments.** Fellow scientists disbelieved him [Halley's comet had not returned]. In any case, he was not far off the mark with the comet as harbinger of cataclysm.

Rudjer Josip Boscovich, 1750, interpreted the 1740 observation of Pierre Bouguer [that gravitational attraction of the Andes, being less than their mass, would indicate that] **the Andes' low density at depth, compensates for its surface mass.** This is the basis for the theory of isostasy (bouyancy of blocks of the crust, where lighter blocks float higher, heavier blocks lower), a major geological idea.

Lomonosov, Mikhail V., 1759, drew the conclusion that topography results from uplift and subsidence, modified by slow processes of erosion. Whereas Charles Lyell (1797-1875) and James Hutton (1726-97) are touted as fathers of modern geology, Lomonosov has a better claim to the title.

Horace, B. de Saussure, 1779, observed in the Alps that **glaciers move by gravity and that erratics and large valleys are the result of violent floodwaters,** common-sense ideas consistent with those presented in this book for other terranes.

Erasmus Darwin, 1794-96, observed that **evolution results from new characteristics that survive and are passed on and that species adapt to their environment by their food gathering abilities,** a theory not unlike that for which Charles claimed credit 65 years later.

James Hutton, 1795, explained that **coastal ocean waves are best at rounding rocks, rivers less so; that sedimentary rock is altered by heat and pressure while buried in the Earth; that glaciers carry blocks of rock great distances; and that rivers wear terrain down to near flatness.** This is just about all there is to gradual geological processes, which Charles Lyell is often given the credit for "fathering" forty years later.

Benjamin Henry Latrobe, 1798, enunciated the first explanation of **the origin of the Pacific basin: the Moon was ejected from it.** He later withdrew from the idea. In 1990 this is a popular scenario among scientists but with a different twist: a cometary impact at an oblique angle of incidence splashed crustal rock into orbit, where it accumulated into the Moon.

Baron Georges Cuvier, 1812, reached the conclusion that **geological history is long and peaceful in the main but punctuated by sudden violent conditions that are effected by no known process.** He went on to point out that, when species were destroyed, new ones, more advanced, appeared in finished form. The essential correctness of these perceptions did not prevent their eclipse for almost 150 years starting in the 1830s, a result of overwhelming popular bias toward exclusive gradualism.

James Hall, 1812, enunciated the idea that **violent uplift of an island with adjoining sea bottom might generate a wave capable of broadcasting erratic boulders across foreign terrain.**

Horace H. Hayden, 1820, expounded the idea that **a flood resultant from rapid melting of the polar ice cap, widely distributed the "drift."**

Jens Esmark, 1824, wrote of **the glacier covering the continent [of Europe].** This seems to be the first espousal of the continental ice sheet theory, although it is unclear whether Hayden conceived of his "polar ice cap" as reaching as far south as middle North America.

Peter Dobson, 1825, described **ice rafting of boulders,** which are carried under water encased in the floating ice.

Leonce E. de Beaumont, 1829, described **mountain building as the result of tangential force caused by a shrinking Earth.** This idea is not supported today; but it held sway up to the 1850s.

Amos Eaton, 1830, described **debris rising from the interior of the Earth as a result of unknown force.**

John F. W. Herschel, 1836, promulgated the idea that plasticity of the crust allows deeply-buried rock to flow outward.

Louis Agassiz, 1837, recognized repeated destruction and creation of species, which he attributed to **climatic change, during which large-scale loss of life occurred. As collective body-heat dissipated, atmospheric temperature fell, and an ice age ensued.** In 1989 environmental scientist David Suzuki, is quoted as being concerned that methane emanations from bovine herds is leading to global warming. The direct contradiction, Agassiz for cooling, Suzuki for warming, is appropriate to demonstrate the nonsense that arises from unfounded speculation.

Since the total heat of bovine herds is trivial in comparison with global heat sinks, these models for global climate change should be treated as the ultimate in absurdity. Perhaps a science fiction writer could extract entertainment value from them.

Global warming as a consequence of the emission of oxides of carbon into the atmosphere, is another alarm that is being spread

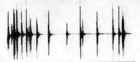

by ill-informed, self-appointed environmental monitors of our day. Their assumption is that atmospheric warming will melt the ice caps, raise sea level, swamp most cities, and engender desertification of marginally-arid farming regions. The exact opposite is at least as likely: that, if global warming occurs, it will raise evaporation, precipitate more snow on the already-expanding ice caps, cause more rainfall, and increase arability and plant growth worldwide.

Richard Owen, 1857, said that **internal forces expand the Earth causing the crust to break up into continents.**

John Wilson Dawson, 1864, enunciated the idea that **the Canadian Plains as well as New England and the Great Lakes areas subsided and were innundated,** whence the "boulder dirt" was deposited.

William Thomson (Lord Kelvin) 1868 thought that **seeds and small insects could have arrived on Earth in meteorites.**

G. K. Gilbert, 1889, said **lunar craters are formed by impact not volcanism.**

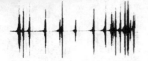

Acknowledgements

The writings of four geologists and three astronomers deserve recognition as sources of inspiration for important elements of my theories.

S. Warren Carey's perception of crustal accretion was not in my purview when I started this book. "Discovering" his ideas has been a revelation and inspiration. Much of what I had already observed neatly fell into place after I read Theories of Earth and Universe (1988).

John W. Gabelman's recognition of diapirism of serpentinized mafic and ultramafic intrusive rock in the California Coast Ranges has become fundamentally important in my thinking, since he brought it to my attention in 1985 in connection with our work in the Klamaths.

J. Budel and C. H. Crickmay separately on landform evolution have furnished me with rationale necessary to my recognition of some cataforms.

S. V. M. Clube and his colleague, Bill Napier, have provided cometary perspective much needed and otherwise unavailable to a geologist.

Sir Fred Hoyle and his colleague, C. Wickramasinghe, have provided rationale for biological evolution in a planetary context. Their theory of viruses from space is a fundamental advance in scientific knowledge. Their insights are important on a wide-ranging list of interdisciplinary topics.

Thomas Gold has furnished rationale for many endogenic processes that I have found invaluable to resolve geological enigmas. His theory of the mechanics involved in the rise of volatiles from mantle depth to the surface is a major new insight into that very important process.

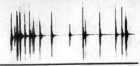

A SUMMATION

I find it remarkable that the originators of these ideas are not all regarded as mainstream thinkers in their fields. In some cases they are not even very well known. In all cases they have dealt first hand with natural phenomena. Those who might be inclined to ignore them or detract from their ideas have usually not done equivalent thinking. Why, I find myself asking, has no petroleum geologist met Tom Gold's proof that petroleum must come from Earth's interior? There is little acceptance among this large professional body of his intriguing and not-weakly-supported idea.

Why do the objectors to the idea of subduction not meet the opposition head-on with counter-evidence? Not only Carey but a large number of highly qualified geologists object. A good sampling is presented in the two-volume forty-paper symposium on plate tectonics alternatives entitled, "Critical aspects of the plate tectonics theory" (Barto-Kyriakidis, ed, 1990).

From the field of my own direct observations, why after 100 years has no one identified the easily-identified lahar character of the Weaverville formation? Why has the equally-easily-identified Calgary Silt not previously been recognized as a torrential flood deposit? Why has no one recognized that Red Rock Pass has conducted water southward into Lake Bonneville's basin? And why does a simple [and wrong] idea like long-distance tranmissibility of compressional force in rock still persist in professional minds, which should know better? The reason for clearly-wrong ideas persisting and of often-eloquently-posed questions going unanswered escapes me.

The interested reader may find more enlightenment in reading the authors and books I have named. He should be admonished to recognize that a science frontier is before us. Gleick (1987) and Davies (1988) demonstrate indisputably that non-linear processes occur widely in our Universe. I think my geological presentations show enigmatical evidence suggesting that non-linear processes are at work. As there is no secure understanding of how to deal with the non-linear or even to recognize the limits of its existence, surprising discoveries could lie ahead.

Research on the high-pressure behavior of carbides, hydrides, hydrocarbons and silanes in deep Earth processes should lead to new understanding of the all-important mechanisms of diapirism, earthquakes, the effusion of volatiles from mantle depths, and the conditions for initiation of mid-crustal melting. The new satellite surveillance systems that are now churning out detailed geodetic data should be a great help in defining the ongoing dilation and relaxation processes that have been difficult to recognize up to our time.

Invasion of metal sponges by hydrogen adds mass to the metal without increasing its volume at surface pressures. Who knows what will be the endpoint of the process at 1.3 million atmospheres pressure? And, if the hydrogen is later scavenged from its hydride association by active carbon and silicon, should we not expect Earth to turn very lively as diapirs emerge due to volume increase? Could there be any doubt that such diapirs would rise bouyantly and bring about all manner of geological processes?

I think that future research is likely to answer all the above questions in the affirmative, that is to say,

DIAPIRISM of variously explosive and quiescent nature will be established as the fundamental process of geological endogeny, just as COMETARY IMPACTS are now recognized as the fundamental agents of exogeny.

DIAPIRS and COMETS are
the ENGINES of VIOLENCE in
our ENVIRONMENT.

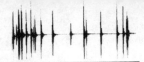

SELECTED REFERENCES

AALTO, K.R., 1988 *"SEDIMENTOLOGY OF THE MONTGOMERY CREEK FORMATION, STASTA COUNTY, CALIFORNIA"* California Geology, v41, #11, p254-259

ALEXANDER, C.M.O'D., ARDEN, J.W., PIER, J., WALKER, R.M., PILLINGER, C.M. 1990 *"ION PROBE STUDIES OF INTERSTELLAR SIC IN ORDINARY CHONDRITES"* XXI Lun. & Plan. Sci. Conf. abstr., pp9-10

ALEXANDER, C.M.O'F., SWAN, P.D., WALKER, R.M., 1990 *"THE DETECTION OF SIC IN SITU IN CM METEORITES"*, XXI Lun. & Plan. Sci. Conf., abstr. pp11-12

ALLEN, J.E., 1983-85, *"TIME TRAVEL IN OREGON"*. A scrapbook of geological articles published in the Portland Oregonian", Portland State Univ. Press

ALT. D., SEARS, J.M., HYNDMAN, D.W., 1988 *"TERRESTRIAL MARIA: THE ORIGINS OF LARGE BASALT PLATEAUS, HOTSPOT TRACKS AND SPREADING RIDGES"* Jour. Geol., v96, pp647-62

ALT, D., & HYNDMAN, D., 1989, *"ROADSIDE GEOLOGY OF IDAHO"* Mountain Press.

ALVAREZ, L.W., ALVAREZ, W., ASARO, F., MICHEL, H. V. 1980, *EXTRATERRESTRIAL CAUSE FOR CRETACEOUS-TERTIARY EXTINCTION"* Science, v298, p1095.

BARTO-KRIAKIDIS, A., ed. 1990 *"CRITICAL ASPECTS OF THE PLATE TECTONICS THEORY"* Two volumes, Theophrastus Publications, SA

BAUER, H. H., 1984, *"BEYOND VELIKOVSKY"*, U. of Ill. Press.

BIRD, J.M., WEATHERS, M.S., 1975 *"TERRESTRIAL OCCURRENCE OF ELEMENTAL SILICON"* Abstr., EOS, v56, p465.

BOHOR, B.F., IZETT, G.A., 1986, *"WORLDWIDE SIZE DISTRIBUTION OF SHOCKED QUARTZ AT THE K/T BOUNDARY: EVIDENCE FOR A NORTH AMERICAN IMPACT SITE"* LPSC XVII Abstr. p68-69

BOHOR, B.F. & TRIPLEHORN, D.M., 1987, *"FLYASH: AN ANALOG FOR SPHERULES IN K/T BOUNDARY CLAYS"* LPSV XVIII, Abstr. p103-4

BOUDIER, F., LE SUEUR, E., NICHOLAS, A., 1989 *"STRUCTURE OF AN ATYPICAL OPHIOLITE: THE TRINITY COMPLEX, EASTERN KLAMATH MOUNTAINS, CALIFORNIA"* GSA v101, #6 pp820-33

BUDEL, J., 1982, *"CLIMATIC GEOMORPHOLOGY"* Princeton U. Press

CAREY, S. WARREN, 1988, *"THEORIES OF EARTH AND UNIVERSE"* Stanford University Press.

CLUBE, S. V. M., 1988(?), *"THE DYNAMICS OF ARMAGEDDON"*, Speculations of Science and Technology, v11, #4, p255.

CLUBE, V., NAPIER, W.M., 1982, *"THE COSMIC SERPENT"* Universe Books

CRANDALL, D.R., 1989, *"GIGANTIC DEBRIS AVALANCHE OF PLEIS-TOCENE AGE FROM ANCESTRAL MOUNT SHASTA VOLCANO, CALIFORNIA"* USGS Bul. 1861

CRICKMAY, C. H., 1974, *"THE WORK OF THE RIVER"* Macmillan Press, London

CRICKMAY, C.H., 1976, *"THE HYPOTHESIS OF UNEQUAL ACTIVITY "* Chapter 6 in "Theories of Landform Development", Publications in Geomorphology, S.U.N.Y., Binghamton, N.Y., U.S.A.

CURRY, R. R., 1977, *"GLACIAL HISTORY OF FLATHEAD VALLEY AND LAKE MISSOULA FLOODS"* in Field Guide 4, Rky. Mtn. Sec., GSA, 30th Ann. Mtg.

DAVIS, G.A., 1966, *"METAMORPHIC AND GRANITIC HISTORY OF THE KLAMATH MOUNTAINS"* in Geology of northern California, Bull. 190, Calif. Div. of Mines & Geology, p39-50

DAVIS, G.A., 1979, *"INTRAPLATE EXTENSIONAL TECTONICS - WESTERN UNITED STATES"* IN RMAG-UGA BASIN & RANGE SYMPOS., G.W. Newman & H.D. Goode, eds.

DAVIS, G.A., MONGER, J.W.H., BURCHFIELD, B.C., 1978, *"MESOZOIC CONSTRUCTION OF THE CORDILLERAN 'COLLAGE', CENTRAL BRITISH COLUMBIA TO CENTRAL CALIFORNIA"* in Howell, D.G. and McDougall, K.A., eds., "Mesozoic paleogeography of the western U.S.: Soc. Econ. Paleontologists and Mineralogists. Pac. Coast section, Paleogeography Symposium 2, pp-33.

DAVIES, P., 1988, *"THE COSMIC BLUEPRINT"* Simon & Schuster

DIETZ, R.S., GRIEVE, R.A.F., 1961, *"VREDEFORT RING STRUCTURE METEORITE IMPACT SCAR"* Jour. Geol. v69, p499

DIKOV, V.P. GERASIMOV, M.V., YAKOVLEV, O.I. 1989 *"SOME PECULIARITIES OF REFRACTORY ELEMENTS, VOLATILIZATION FROM SILICATE MELTS"* Abstr. Lun. & Plan. Sci. Conf. XX, p244

FOSTER, D.A., HYNDMAN, D.W., 1990, *"LARGE-SCALE CRUSTAL ANATEXIS: THE IMPORTANCE OF SUBCRUSTAL MAGMA INTRUSION"* EOS, v71, #9 pp299-300

FRANK L., YEATES, C., 1988, *"COMET CONTROVERSEY CAUGHT ON FILM"*, Science News, v133, p340.

FUIS, G.S., ZUCCA, J.J., MOONEY, W.D., MILDERREIT, B., 1987, *"GEOLOGICAL INTERPRETATION OF SEISMIC REFRACTION RESULTS IN NORTHEASTERN CALIFORNIA"*, Bull. GSA v98, #1

GABELMAN, J.W., 1984, *"CIRCULAR GEOMORPHIC FEATURES PERMISSIVE TO INTERPRETATION AS CONDUITS OF MANTLE DEGASSING"* Global Tectonics and Metallogeny, v2, #3-4, p151.

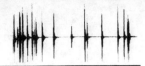

GANAPATHY, R., 1982, *"EVIDENCE OF A MAJOR METEORITE IMPACT ON THE EARTH 34 MILLION YEARS AGO: IMPLICATION FOR EOCENE EXTINCTIONS"* Science, v216, p885.

GILMOUR, I., GUENTHER, F., 1988, *"THE GLOBAL CRETACEOUS-TERTIARY FIRE: BIOMASS OR FOSSIL CARBON"* Lun. & Plan. Inst., Global Catastrophes in Earth History Conf., pp60-61.

GLASS, B. P., 1986, *"TEKTITES AND MICROTEKTITES: KEY FACTS AND INFERENCES,"* Workshop on Cryptoexplosions and Catastrophes in the Geological Record, Parys, RSA, 1986, working papers.

GLEICK, J., 1987, *"CHAOS: MAKING A NEW SCIENCE"* Penguin Books.

GOLD, T., 1987, *"POWER FROM THE EARTH"* J.M. Dent & Sons.

GRAUP, G., 1987, *"A VOLCANIC AEROSOL FOR THE CRETACEOUS-TERTIARY EVENTS - RESULTS FROM THE LATTENGEBIRGE SECTION, BAVARIAN ALPS"* Workshop on Cryptoexplosions and Catastrophes in the Geological Record, Parys, RSA, working papers.

GRAUP, G., SPETTEL, B., 1989, *"MINERALOGY AND PHASE-CHEMISTRY OF AN IR-ENRICHED PRE-K/T LAYER FROM THE LATTENGEBIRGE, BAVARIAN ALPS, AND SIGNIFICANCE FOR KTB PROBLEM"* Earth & Sci. Let. 95 pp271-290.

GRIEVE, R.A.F., ROBERTSON, P.B., 1987, *"TERRESTRIAL IMPACT STRUC-TURES"*, Geol. Surv. Can., Map 1658A.

GRINNEL, G., 1976, *"THE ORIGINS OF MODERN GEOLOGICAL THEORY "* Kronos, v1, # 4.

HAKE, B.F., WILLIS, R., & ADDISON, C.C., 1942, *"FOLDED THRUST FAULTS IN THE FOOTHILLS OF ALBERTA"* Bull. Geol. Soc. Am. v53, #2, p291.

HANSEN, H.J., RASMUSSEN, K.L., GWONTZ, R., KUNZENDORF, H., 1987 *"IRIDIUM-BEARING CARBON BLACK AT THE CRETACEOUS-TERTIARY BOUNDARY "* Bull. of Geol. Soc. of Denmark, v36, pp305-314.

HIGINBOTHAM, L., 1987, *"MONTGOMERY CREEK FORMATION, KLAMATH MOUNTAINS, SHASTA COUNTY, CALIFORNIA"* California Geology, v40, #6, p130-138.

HINDS, N.E.A., 1933, *"GEOLOGIC FORMATIONS OF THE REDDING-WEAVERVILLE DIST."* CA. Jour. Mines & Geol., v29, #1-2, p76.

HOYLE, F., WICKRAMASINGHE, C., 1978, *"COMETS, ICE AGES, AND ECOLOGICAL CATASTROPHES"* Astrophys. Space Sci., 53, p523.

HOYLE, F., 1981, *"ICE: THE ULTIMATE HUMAN CATASTROPHE"* Continuum Publishing Co.

HOYLE, F., 1983, *"THE INTELLIGENT UNIVERSE"*, Holt, Rinehart & Winston.

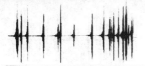
HOYLE, F., WICKRAMASINGHE, C., 1985, *"LIVING COMETS"* U. Col: Cardiff Press.

HSU, H.J., 1967, *"ORIGIN OF LARGE OVERTURNED SLABS OF APENNINES, ITALY "* AAPG Bull. v51, #1.

HUBBERT, M.K. & RUBEY, W.W., 1959, *"ROLE OF FLUID PRESSURE IN MECHANICS OF OVERTHRUST FAULTING"* Bull. Geo. Soc. Am., v70, p115.

HUNT, C.B., ed. 1981, *"PLEISTOCENE LAKE BONNEVILLE, AS DESCRIBED IN THE NOTEBOOKS OF G.K. GILBERT"*, 1875-1880, B.Y. UNIV. Geol. Ser., v29, Pt. 1.

HUNT, C.B., 1979, *"HYPOTHESES OF HISTORY OF GREAT BASIN"* in RMAG-UGA 979 Basin and Range Sympos., G.W. Newman & H.D. Goode, eds., p1.

HUNT, C.W., 1977, *"INNUNDATION TOPOGRAPHY OF THE COLUMBIA RIVER SYSTEM "* Bull. Can. Soc. of Petroleum Geol., v25, #3.

HUNT C.W., 1979, *"CATASTROPHIC TERMINATION OF THE LAST WISCONSIN ICE ADVANCE, OBSERVATIONS IN ALBERTA AND IDAHO"* Bull. Can. Soc. of Petroleum Geol., 25, #3.

IRWIN, W.P., 1966, *"GEOLOGY OF THE KLAMATH MOUNTAINS PROVINCE"* in GEOLOGY OF NORTHERN CALIFORNIA: Calif. Div. Mines & Geology, Bull. 190, pp19-38.

IRWIN, W.P., *"TECTONIC ACCRETION OF THE KLAMATH MOUNTAINS"* in Ernst, W.G., ed. *"THE GEOTECTONIC DEVELOPMENT OF CALIFORNIA"*: Rubey v1, pp29-49, Prentice Hall, Inc.

JARRATT, R.D., MALDE, R.E., 1987, *"PALEODISCHARGE OF LATE PLEISTOCENE BONNEVILLE FLOOD IN THE SNAKE RIVER BASIN, IDAHO"* GSA v99, #1, p127.

KELLER, G. 1989, *"EXTENDED CRETACEOUS/TERTIARY BOUNDARY EXTINCTIONS AND DELAYED POPULATION CHANGE IN PLANKTONIC FORAMINIFERA FROM BRAZOS RIVER, TEXAS"* abstr. EOS, v70, #16.

KOLESNIKOV, E.M., 1988, *"ISOTOPIC INVESTIGATIONS IN THE AREA OF THE TUNGUSKA CATASTROPHE IN THE YEAR 1908"* Abstr. p97, Lunar Plan. Sci. Conf. on Global Catastrophes in Earth History, Snowbird, Utah, Oct. 20-23, 1988.

LABERGE, G.L., 1989, *"A MODEL FOR THE BIOLOGICAL PRECIPITATION OF PRECAMBRIAN IRON-FORMATION"* Workshop on Early Crustal Genesis: The World's Oldest Rocks, Lun. & Plan. Inst. Tech. Rept. 86-04, p71.

LINDSLEY-GRIFFIN, N. 1982, *"PLAEOGEOGRAPHIC IMPLICATIONS OF OPHIOLITES IN THE ORDOVICIAN TRINITY COMPLEX, KLAMATH MOUNTAINS, CALIFORNIA"* in Steward, J.H. et al, eds. SEPM, Pacific Coast Paleogeography Symposium.

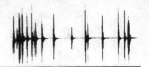

LYDON, P.A. & KLEIN, I.E., 1969, "GEOLOGY OF THE SE QUARTER OF THE TRINITY LAKE QUADRANGLE, TRINITY COUNTY, CALIFORNIA" Calif. Division of Mines, Map sheet 12.

MALDE, H.E., 1968, "THE CATASTAOPHIC LATE PLEISTOCENE BON-NEVILLE FLOOD IN THE SNAKE RIVER PLAIN, IDAHO" USGS Prof. Pap. 596.

MANKINEN, E.A., IRWIN, W.P., & GROMME, C.S., 1989, "PALEOMAGNE-TIC STUDY OF THE EASTERN KLAMATH TERRANE, CALIFORNIA, AND IMPLICATIONS FOR THE TECTONIC HISTORY OF THE KLAMATH MOUNTAINS PROVINCE", Abstr. EOS, July 18, 1989.

MARGULIS, L., & SAGAN, D., 1986, "MICRO-COSMOS", Summit Books.

MITCHELL, G.C., 1979, "STRATIGRAPHY AND REGIONAL IMPLICATIONS OF THE ARGONAUT ENERGY NO. 1, FEDERAL, MILLARD COUNTY, UTAH" IN RMAG-UGA-1979 Basin and Range Symposium, G.W. Newman & H.D. Goode, eds.

NORRELL, G.T., TAIXELL, A., HARPER, G.D., 1989, "MICROSTRUCTURE OF SERPENTINITE MYLONITES FROM THE JOSEPHINE OPHIOLITE AND SERPENTINIZATION IN RETROGRESSIVE SHEAR ZONES, CALIFORNIA" GSA v101, #5, pp673-82.

OFFICER, C.B., HALLAM, A., DRAKE, C.L., DEVINE, J.D. 1987, "THE LATE CRETACEOUS AND PAROXYSMAL CRETACEOUS/TERTIARY EX-TINCTIONS" Nature, v326, #6109, p143-149.

PARDEE, J.T., 1910, "THE GLACIAL LAKE MISSOULA" Jour. Geol, v18.

PATTEN, D.W., 1966, "THE BIBLICAL FLOOD AND THE ICE EPOCH" Pacific Meridian Publishing.

POHL, J. 1987, "INTRODUCTION TO THE RIES CRATER" Workshop on Cryp-toexplosions, Parys, South Africa, July 6-10, 1987.

RICE, A. R., 1988, "DYNAMICS OF EXPLODING MAGMA CHAMBERS: IM-PLICATIONS FOR K/T VOLCANISM AND MASS EXTINCTIONS" Abstr. p154 Lun. & Plan. Inst., Conference on Global Catastrophes in Earth History, Snowbird, Utah, Oct. 20-23, 1988.

RICE, A.R. 1989, "SNOWBIRD II: A DISSENTING VIEW" Science, v243 p875-87y.

ROBERTS, R.J., RADKE, A.S., 7 COATS, R.R., 1971, "GOLD-BEARING DE-POSITS IN NORTH-CENTRAL NEVADA AND SOUTHWESTERN IDAHO" Soc. Ec. Geol. v66, pp14-33.

SCHAFFER, J.P., 1977, "PLEISTOCENE LAKE YOSEMITE AND THE WISCON-SIN GLACIATION OF YOSEMITE VALLEY " CA GVOL.

SCOTT, W.E., PIERCE, K.L., BRADBURY, J.P., FORESTER, R.M., 1982 "RE-VISED QUATERNARY STRATIGRAPHY AND CHRONOLOGY IN THE AMERICAN FALLS AREA, SOUTHEAST IDAHO", Idaho Bur. Mines, Bull. 26, p581.

SHAW, J., 1989, *"DRUMLINS, SUBGLACIAL MELTWATER FLOODS, AND OCEAN RESPONSES"*, Geology, v17, p853-6.

SHOEMAKER, E.M., 1988, *"ASTEROID AND COMET FLUX IN THE NEIGHBORHOOD OF THE EARTH"* Abstr., P174, Lunar Plan. Sci., Conf. on Global Catastrophes in Earth History, Snowbird, Utah Oct. 20-23, 1988.

STOKES, W.L., 1979, *"PALEOHYDROLOGY OF THE GREAT BASIN"* in RMAG-UGA 1979 Basin and Range Synpos., G. W. Newman & H.D. Goode, eds. p345.

SUGDEN, D.E., JOHN, B.S., 1976, *"GLACIERS AND LANDSCAPE"* Halstead Press.

TEMPLE, P.G., 1968, *"MECHANICS OF LARGE-SCALE GRAVITY SLIDING IN THE GREEK PELOPONNESOS"* GSA v79, #6.

THOMPSON, S.J., 1988, *"A CHRONOLOGY OF GEOLOGICAL THINKING FROM ANTIQUITY TO 1899"* Scarecrow Press, Inc.

TOUTAIN, J.P., MEYER, G. 1989, *"IRIDIUM-BEARING SUBLIMATES AT A HOT-SPOT VOLCANO (PITON DE LA FOURNAISE, INDIAN OCEAN)"*, Geoph. Res. Let., v16, #12, p1391-4.

TREDOUX, M., DEWIT, M.J., HART, R.J., LINDSAY, N.M., & SELLSCHOP, J.P.F., 1987, *"CHEMOSTRATIGRAPHY ACROSS THE CRETACEOUS-TERTIARY BOUNDARY AT LOCALITIES IN DENMARK AND NEW ZEALAND: A CASE FOR TERRESTRIAL ORIGIN OF THE PLATINUM GROUP ELEMENT ANOMALY "*, Workshop on cryptoexplosions, Parys, South Africa, July 6-10, 1987.

TRIMBLE, D.E., CARR, W.J., 1961, *"LATE QUATERNARY HISTORY OF THE SNAKE RIVER IN THE AMERICAN FALLS REGION, IDAHO"* GSA Bull. v.72, p1739.

VELIKOVSKY, I., 1950, *"WORLDS IN COLLISION"*, Doubleday.

VON ENGLEHARDT, W., 1987, *"RIES CRATER, GERMANY: REVIEW OF SHOCK METAMORPHISM AND BRECCIA TYPES"* Workshop on Cryptoexplosions and Catastrophes in the Geological Record, Parys, South Africa, July 6-10, 1987.

WAGNER, D.L. & SAUCEDO, G.J., 1987, *"GEOLOGY OF THE WEED QUADRANGLE"* Calif. Div. of Mines.

WAITT, R.B., 1985, *"CASE FOR PERIODIC, COLOSSAL JÖKULHLAUPS FROM PLEISTOCENE GLACIAL LAKE MISSOULA"* GSA Bull. v96, p1271.

WASHKIN, M., 1985, *"MRS. O'LEARY'S COMET"*, Academy Chicago Publishers.

WHEELER, H.E., & COOK, E.F., 1954, *"STRUCTURAL AND STRATIGRAPHIC SIGNIFICANCE OF THE SNAKE RIVER CAPTURE, IDAHO-OREGON"* Jour. Geol. v62, No. 6.

WHITE, J.M., MATHEWES, R.W., MATHEWS, W.H., 1979, *"RADIOCARBON DATES FROM BOONE LAKE AND THEIR RELATION TO THE 'ICE-FREE CORRIDOR' IN THE PEACE RIVER DISTRICT, ALBERTA, CANADA"* Can. Jour. Earth Sci. v16, #9, p1870-4.

INDEX

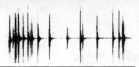

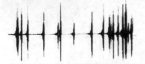

A Thumbnail Glossary for Non-Geologists

A

Allocthon - A rock mass displaced from its origin by tectonics
Astrobleme - A crater resulting from impact (p. 8)

B

Bolide - A projectile

C

Carbonatite - An alkaline igneous rock
Chrondritic - Stony
Clastic, clast - "Broken" rock fragments, broken pieces
Coesite - A high-pressure form of silica

D

Décollement - A detachment plane, usually nearly horizontal
Dextral motion - "Right-handed", opposite side moves right
Diapir - An up-thrust rock plug that breaches cover rock
Dike - A tabular intrusive body of rock
Dip - The down-slope direction of an inclined plane
Drag fold - A sympathetic fold induced by adjacent fault motion
Drift - Deposits of glaciers or waters emanating from glaciers
Drumlin (-field) - Elongate mounding of gravel or till shaped by torrential water flow, normally under-ice flow
Dunite - A rock of the peridotite group

E

E/O - Eocene to Oligocene transition period

F

Foliation - Planar arrangement of tectural or structural features

G

Gabbro - A mafic rock (having little silica)
Gastrobleme - A crater caused by deep-Earth explosion (endogeny, p. 8)
Graben - A down-faulted block
Granite, -oid - Quartz-rich crystalline igneous rock

H

Hanging wall - That side of a fault that is above the other side
Harzburgite - A rock of the peridotite group

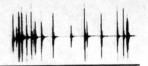

H

Isostasy - Crustal blocks "floating" on mantle assume elevations according to inverse function of density

J

J/K - Jurassic to Cretaceous transition, "Nevadan revolution"
Jökulhlaup - An outburst of water after containment under a glacier

K

Kimberlite - A chaotic peridotite of probable mantle origin
K/T - Cretaceous to Tertiary transition period

L

Lahar - A mudflow of chiefly volcanic debris
Lamprophyre - Rock comprising mafic minerals in a mixed mafic-feldspathic matrix

M

Mafic - Iron and magnesium-bearing minerals
Magma - A rock melt, sometimes with suspended solids
Mantle - The shell of Earth beneath the crust
Mantle plume - A place of upward mantle movement
Mantle-type crust - Ultramafic, syn. "oceanic crust"
Mass wasting - Downslope slumpage of soil and loose rock
Melange - Chaotic blocks of diverse rock types and origins
Metamorphic rocks - Rocks recrystallized by high temperature/pressure
Migmatite - A composite rock of igneous and metamorphic components
Miogeosyncline - A depression receiving sedimentation without volcanics
Moldavites - Tektites of one of four strewnfields of the world
myBP - Millions of years before present
Mylonite - Dynamically metamorphosed finely-crystalline rock

N

Nappe - An allocthonous rock slab
Normal fault - A fault of steep dip and down-dropped hanging wall

O

Olistostrome - A chaotic, submarine slump in bed or lens form
Ophiolite sequence - Peridotite overlain by mafic and ultramafic rock, a dike complex, pillow lavas, and sediments in that order
Orocline - A change of direction of a mountain belt
Orogen, -esis - A belt of mountain building deformation, -the process
Overthrust - A low-dip fault with older rocks overriding younger

P,Q

Peneplain - A low-lying, almost-plane featureless land surface

Peridotite - Rock made up of olivine and accessory minerals but lacking in feldspars

Pillow lava - A submarine volcanic rock

Plate tectonics - A theory of Earth crust comprising plates that move around impelled by convecting mantle plumes

Pluton - An igneous body that crystallized at depth

Pseudotachylite - A melt rock with entrained solid fragments that resembles rock melted by contact with magma

R,S

Rhythmite - Sedimentation repeated after sub-equal time intervals

Schist - A strongly foliated, crystalline metamorphic rock

Serpentine, -ite - A group of hydrous silicate minerals

Siderophile - "Moon-loving", not naturally found on Earth surface

Silanes - Silicon hydrides of general formula Si_nH_{2n+2}

Sinistral motion - "Left-handed", opposite side moves left

Sole fault - The bottom fault in an overthrust series

Strike-slip fault - A fault with horizontal displacement primarily

Surge cloud - A high-speed explosive volcanic exhalation

Subduction - Crustal materials circulating downward in response to underlying convecting mantle plume

Suevite - Page 25 (type locality is described in text)

Stishevite - A high-pressure form of silica

T

Tectonism, -ics - Structure-producing crustal movement, -the forces of

Tektites - Page 27 (treated in text)

Till, -ite - Unsorted, sub-glacier deposit, -lithified form

Tsunami - A wave caused by disturbance of the seafloor

Turbidite - A submarine debris flow

U,V

Ultramafic - A rock almost exclusively made up of mafic minerals

Varve, -ing - Thin-layered sedimentation indicating annual cycles

W, X,Y, Z

yBP - Years before present